CHRISTMAS WITH

CHRISTMAS WITH ELVIS

THE OFFICIAL GUIDE TO THE HOLIDAYS
FROM THE
KING OF ROCK 'N' ROLL

ROBERT K. ELDER

Running Press
PHILADELPHIA

Running Press
Hachette Book Group
1290 Avenue of the Americas, New York, NY 10104
www.runningpress.com
@Running_Press

Printed in China

First Edition: October 2021

Published by Running Press, an imprint of Perseus Books, LLC, a subsidiary of
Hachette Book Group, Inc. The Running Press name and logo is a trademark
of the Hachette Book Group.

The Hachette Speakers Bureau provides a wide range of authors for speaking events.
To find out more, go to www.hachettespeakersbureau.com or call (866) 376-6591.

The publisher is not responsible for websites (or their content)
that are not owned by the publisher.

Print book cover and interior design by Amanda Richmond.
Illustrations by Chris King

Library of Congress Control Number: 2020947214

ISBNs: 978-0-7624-6976-5 (hardcover), 978-0-7624-6977-2 (ebook)

1010

10 9 8 7 6 5 4 3 2 1

TO MY PARENTS,
from whom I inherited a love
of both Christmas and Elvis

Contents

✦ INTRODUCTION ✦

Kids love Christmas, and Elvis was always a big kid at heart.

To Elvis, Christmas at Graceland was a time for family and friends, a respite from the road and the recording studio. It was a time to sing gospel songs around the piano and give out extravagant gifts.

All of this was in contrast to Elvis' poor roots in Tupelo, Mississippi, where money was tight and his family was forced out of the two-room house where he was born, when his father couldn't continue the payments.

"My Mama and I used to plan Christmas for days, even when we had no money at all," Elvis remembered. "We weren't the only family who was thankful to have a Christmas basket of groceries."

Christmas remained his favorite holiday, and some of his first performances were in Christmas plays in fifth and sixth grade. It was the holiday closest to Elvis' heart.

"I believed in Santa Claus until I was eight years old. Some of the kids at school told me there was no such thing. Mama explained it to me in such a way that Christmas didn't lose its magic," Elvis said in 1961.

When Elvis finally became "Elvis" and started dyeing those dirty-blond locks jet black, he gave out more than Cadillacs. When he had money, his friends had money. And Christmas was special—an opportunity to give out hand-picked gifts and be himself with friends and family. "It was like being in fairyland and Santa Claus was my first cousin," remembered Billy Smith, Presley's cousin, about Christmas celebrations at Graceland.

But lavish decorations and gifts were beside the point, he told Jim Kingsley of the *Memphis Commercial Appeal Mid-South Magazine* in 1966.

"There is a lot of difference in Christmases today and when we were growing up in East Tupelo," Elvis said. "[But] honestly, I can't say these are any better. We are just in a better position to spend. But that's not the important thing. It's the friendships and the devotion that really count. Everything is so dreamy when you are young. After you grow up it kind of becomes—just real."

On the following pages we look at the holiday music Elvis recorded and its roots. We also dig into the archives and tell some of the Elvis' favorite holiday stories and memories. And just like at a Christmas party the King of Rock 'n' Roll himself would have loved, we've even brought out a few Yuletide desserts and cocktails and left a few cookies on the plate for Santa.

Whether your Christmas is blue or white, we hope you'll enjoy this very Elvis Christmas.

Robert K. Elder
Chicagoland, 2021

"I'd like to tell everybody that they've made this the best Christmas that I've ever had. We'd like to thank everybody for all the presents and Christmas cards and birthday cards that came in. I got exactly 282 teddy bears during the Christmas holidays. We have the walls lined with them. I'd like to tell you that we deeply appreciate it—that we're sorry we couldn't give everyone a new Lincoln, but they wouldn't sell us that many!"

(ELVIS ON *THE ED SULLIVAN SHOW*, JANUARY 6, 1957)

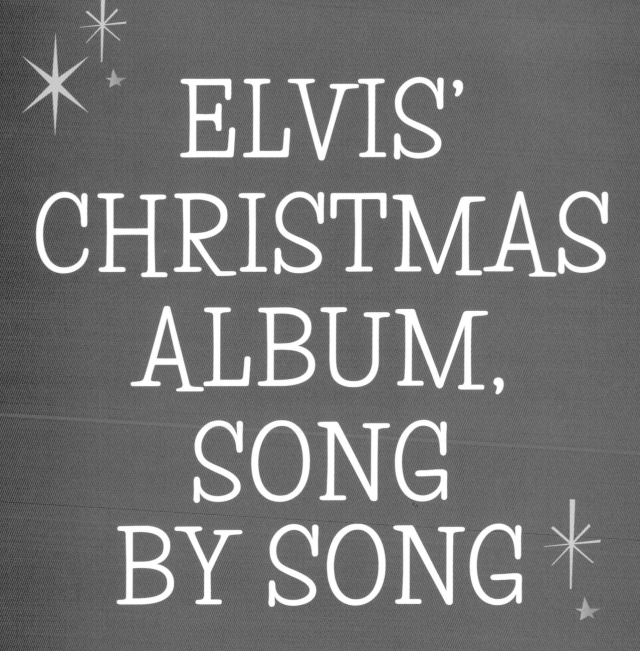

STRICTLY SPEAKING, ELVIS RECORDED ONLY TWO CHRISTMAS albums during his lifetime. That's it. About two dozen tracks from *Elvis' Christmas Album* (October 1957) and *Elvis Sings the Wonderful World of Christmas* (October 1971). And even on the first 1957 holiday offering, four of those songs were taken from his gospel EP *Peace in the Valley* (April 1957). There were assorted singles and EPs, but the core of Elvis' Christmas canon was collected on these two albums, released fourteen years apart.

And the recording sessions—driven by commercial concerns and marred by professional doubt—weren't always easy, as you will learn in the pages to come. Yet these songs have endured because they carry Elvis' undeniable spark and boundless energy. Even the hymns still sound alive, a showcase for Presley's range and vocal presence.

While Elvis covered a lot of holiday standards, he and his songwriters added some originals to the holiday airwaves, notably "Santa Claus Is Back in Town" and "If Every Day Was Like Christmas." Today, along with his rendition of "Blue Christmas," they get abundant holiday airtime and have been remixed and repackaged endlessly.

One holiday album, *If Every Day Was Like Christmas* (1994), came with a special edition pop-up model of Graceland. In 2008, RCA brought in contemporary artists, including Martina McBride and Carrie Underwood, to sing along with Elvis on *Christmas Duets*. Elvis' holiday tracks were even reimagined and reengineered—complete with strings—for *Christmas with Elvis and the Royal Philharmonic Orchestra* in 2017.

As evidenced by this book, Elvis' holiday appeal is as enduring as the songs themselves.

ELVIS' CHRISTMAS ALBUM (October 1957)

Elvis' first holiday record proved to be a tough recording session—even though he was only recording eight tracks for the full LP. The rest of the album would be rounded out by songs from his gospel EP, the four-song *Peace in the Valley* released in April of 1957. Those songs—"(There'll Be) Peace in the Valley (For Me)," "It Is No Secret (What God Can Do)," "I Believe," and "Take My Hand, Precious Lord" (sometimes credited as "Precious Lord Take My Hand")—would amplify his love of religious music and help reshape his image.

But the sessions weren't always a picnic. His producers struggled to find the right material and Elvis ran the risk of further offending the recording establishment, as he was covering three songs made famous by Bing Crosby.

Elvis was attempting to carve out his own niche in a crowded holiday music market, but upon release some stations were refusing to play *Elvis' Christmas Album*. Dick Whittinghill, a DJ at KMPC in Los Angeles, said that despite getting requests to play songs from the album, he put his foot down. Whittinghill said, "That's like having Tempest Storm give Christmas gifts to my kids." (Tempest Storm was known as "the Queen of Exotic Dancers.")

Some critics railed at changes in the musical landscape and the transforming power rock 'n' roll seemed to have over the youth of 1957. "If the carolers outside your door this Christmas season come decked out in dovetail haircuts and Victorian sideburns, you'll know that Elvis Presley's latest album has had its usual fallout effect on the nation's teen-agers," wrote Associated Press feature writer Hugh Mulligan.

Mulligan preferred the offerings by Frank Sinatra, Perry Como, and the Strasbourg Cathedral Choir. Comparing Elvis' efforts on his first Christmas record to these standards, Mulligan wrote, "As Samuel Johnson might have put it: The wonder is not that he did it badly but that he did it at all."

Yet the album worked. Despite the fact that Elvis' Christmas debut "had been so roundly reviled by the critics," as biographer Peter Guralnick wrote, his fans stood up for him. On December 8, 1957, *Miami Herald* columnist Gwen Harrison gave over her Tops in Pops column to fans, after she wrote a particularly scathing review of *Elvis' Christmas Album*. The editor's note recorded that Harrison had "unwittingly walked into a hornet's nest," especially when Harrison's review went off the rails and attacked Elvis' complexion and noted that "though his lipstick and nail polish didn't match" in the album's photographs, "his make-up mercifully hid the pimples that show up in some former photos."

Mrs. Agnes of Miami Beach was among those who came to Elvis' defense, writing: "That boy is a good boy. Why don't they go after some of the kings and queens of Hollywood, some with five or six divorces to their disgrace? . . . But a kid like Elvis, every move he makes they put a bad meaning to it and broadcast it. Newspaper men and women write the most fool things. . . . Elvis has a fine broad pair of shoulders and I guess he can stand all the fool stuff that is written."

Elvis' Christmas Album became a perennial best seller, despite selling only two hundred thousand copies in its first pressing. It came with a booklet of glossy photos promoting Elvis' third movie, *Jailhouse Rock*.

"Taking into account its many later-day variants and iterations, [*Elvis' Christmas Album*] became probably the steadiest long-term seller of Elvis' career," according to Guralnick and Ernst Jorgensen in their discography accompanying *The Complete Elvis Presley Masters Collection* box set.

By contrast, the EP *Elvis Sings Christmas Songs*—released the same week in October 1957—sold a half million copies. The EP featured only four of the modern songs, "suggesting that many teenagers either still didn't own long playing phonographs or couldn't afford the higher purchase price of the album," wrote Guralnick and Jorgensen.

In 2013, *Elvis' Christmas Album* received the Diamond Award from the Recording Industry Association of America, which marked ten million in domestic sales for the album.

TRACK LIST
ELVIS' CHRISTMAS ALBUM

SIDE 1

1. "Santa Claus Is Back in Town"
2. "White Christmas"
3. "Here Comes Santa Claus"
4. "I'll Be Home for Christmas"
5. "Blue Christmas"
6. "Santa Bring My Baby Back (To Me)"

SIDE 2

1. "O Little Town of Bethlehem"
2. "Silent Night"
3. "(There'll Be) Peace in the Valley (For Me)"
4. "I Believe"
5. "Take My Hand, Precious Lord"
6. "It Is No Secret (What God Can Do)"

"Santa Claus Is Back in Town"

WRITTEN BY JERRY LEIBER AND MIKE STOLLER | RECORDED SEPTEMBER 7, 1957

Elvis' first Christmas album was already underway when songwriters Jerry Leiber and Mike Stoller were summoned to the recording session. The songwriting pair had already proved their chemistry with Elvis, who had just recorded hit versions of their songs "Hound Dog," "Love Me," and "Jailhouse Rock."

When Leiber and Stoller entered the Radio Recorders studio in Los Angeles, a smiling Presley greeted them, "My good luck charms are back!" Presley's manager, Colonel Tom Parker, was less cheerful.

"Where's the song?" Parker asked.

But there was no song. They had just driven to the studio after getting a call from Freddy Bienstock, the music wrangler in charge of choosing Elvis' recording catalog.

"Write it now," Parker scowled.

So Lieber and Stoller hid themselves in a closet-like mixing room with an upright piano. Deciding to go with a straight-ahead, twelve-bar blues structure, Stoller pounded out the music while Lieber started singing the line "Hang up your pretty stockings . . ." And the song was finished within eight to fifteen minutes, depending on which songwriter was telling the story. When the partners emerged, Lieber said, "Okay, we got it."

"What took you so long?" Parker growled.

"Writer's block," Lieber said, but the joke didn't crack the Colonel's stony facade.

When Lieber and Stoller played the song for Elvis—originally titled "Christmas Blues"—they could tell Parker thought it was too bluesy for Elvis' inaugural holiday record. But before Parker could object, Elvis said, "Now that's what I call a great goddamn Christmas song! I told you these guys would come through."

Elvis recorded the song in just a few takes and Lieber and Stoller's last-minute addition ended up leading off the album. The song's sexy swagger took Santa out of his sleigh and put him into a big, black Cadillac.

"At first, people were shocked," remembered his longtime drummer, D. J. Fontana. "He was a little ahead of his time, especially on the rock 'n' roll-style Christmas things he did." Elvis stuffed some innuendo and playfulness into the song, making the listener wonder what, exactly, Santa was back in town for. Elvis' suggestive delivery of the line about "coming down your chimney tonight" was certainly enough to get him put on the Naughty List.

"For me, 'Santa Claus Is Back in Town' lives on as one of Elvis' great blues performances," Lieber later said. "It took him back to his Beale Street roots, a place where he was always comfortable."

ACTOR KURT RUSSELL WOULD COVER "SANTA CLAUS IS BACK IN TOWN" FOR the 2018 Netflix movie *The Christmas Chronicles*. This wouldn't be Russell's first run-in with the King of Rock 'n' Roll. At age ten, Russell had one of his first acting jobs working on-screen with Presley in 1963's *It Happened at the World's Fair*. Russell has two short scenes with the young Presley and kicks him in the shins—twice.

"We had a great time, working on that picture. We were on location at the Seattle World's Fair . . . but I noticed crowds of girls flocking to the set. It was my first time seeing an actual mob scene. It was bizarre," Russell later told Turner Classic Movies. "He was not just any singer, he was *the* singer of the twentieth century. His personality, his sex appeal, and his singing style honestly transformed American culture. He just had so much energy."

Later, in 1979, Russell would play Elvis in the TV movie *Elvis*, directed by John Carpenter. If that weren't enough, he would play an Elvis impersonator in *3000 Miles to Graceland* (2001), wherein his character is kicked in the shins by a small boy—a nod to his screen time with Presley.

"White Christmas"

WRITTEN BY IRVING BERLIN | RECORDED SEPTEMBER 6, 1957

Covering this Irving Berlin song, made into a blockbuster classic in 1942 by Bing Crosby, was a risky proposition. Crosby's "White Christmas" was an omnipresent holiday hit, and covering it was tantamount to Presley swiveling his hips over hallowed ground.

In his biography *As Thousands Cheer: The Life of Irving Berlin*, writer Laurence Bergreen tells the story of Berlin hearing the Presley cover for the first time.

"He immediately ordered his staff to telephone radio stations across the country to ask them not to play this barbaric rock-and-roll version," Bergreen wrote.

On December 3, the Associated Press newswire circulated the story that disc jockey Al Priddy had been fired for playing Elvis' "White Christmas," which KEX, his radio station in Portland, Oregon, had banned. The song "is not in the good taste we ascribe to Christmas music," said manager Mel Bailey. "Presley gives it a rhythm and blues interpretation. It doesn't seem to me to be in keeping with the intent of the song."

The story of Berlin's rage and the fired DJ has been repeated (notably in the liner notes of 1994's *If Every Day Was Like Christmas*), although there have been questions about the tale's veracity. As Elvis researcher Shane Brown pointed out, there's little evidence in the press or the music trades of this ever happening.

"We don't question these stories until something suddenly makes it fall apart—and the thing that makes it fall apart is that there is no mention of it until 1990," Brown wrote.

It didn't help that, according to Elvis scholar Johnny Saulovich, "thirty years later, Priddy more-or-less admitted the entire thing had been a publicity stunt, and never stopped drawing a salary."

It's worth mentioning here that Elvis seems to have been inspired by the Drifters' 1954 version of "White Christmas." Strangely, Atlantic Records executive Jerry Wexler reports that when he took the Drifters' cover to Berlin for approval, "Berlin had no objection to the record."

Side note: If you listen closely to Elvis' version, you can hear the piano line end with a few notes from "Jingle Bells."

WHAT CHRISTMAS PRESENTS DID ELVIS BUY FOR HIMSELF?

In 1955, just as he was climbing to the peak of his fame, Elvis bought himself a Martin 000-18 "parlor" guitar. The price? $79.50—not counting the $8 in trade-in credit for his old guitar that the salesman at O. K. Houck Piano Company in Memphis gave him.

Almost two decades later, Elvis was a little more generous with himself and bought a gargantuan diamond ring, which can be seen in 1973's *Aloha from Hawaii via Satellite* concert special. The massive piece of kingly jewelry had an 11½-carat diamond in the center, encircled by other diamonds. Elvis did not say what he paid for it.

"It was a Christmas present to myself," Elvis told a Las Vegas audience. "I was looking for gifts for my father, my grandmother, and my daughter, and when the jeweler came—this just accidentally fell from his case. I was really suckered into buying it. It's the biggest diamond I've ever seen—I just thought I deserved it."

IN 1965, THE GRACELAND GROUNDS WERE DECORATED WITH A FULL-SIZE FIBERGLASS nativity scene, created by Memphis artist Hardie (sometimes spelled "Hardy") Phipps. Elvis' father, Vernon, paid $1,140 to rent the display, which featured a large three-piece stable set, plus nine figures: baby Jesus, Mary, Joseph, three wise men, an angel, and a couple of sheep. The Presleys loved the display so much that Elvis and Priscilla posed in front of the scene for their 1965 Christmas card.

The original set sold on eBay a few years ago, but a larger-than-life set that Elvis ordered in the late 1960s gets displayed at Graceland each year.

Elvis loved the blue Christmas lights that lined Graceland's long driveway every holiday season.

"Confused local pilots sometimes thought they were looking at a landing strip when they flew over the house," said friend George Klein.

"Here Comes Santa Claus"

WRITTEN BY GENE AUTRY AND OAKLEY HALDEMAN | RECORDED SEPTEMBER 6, 1957

Elvis was a huge fan of Westerns, so perhaps it's fitting that he'd cover gentleman cowboy Gene Autry's "Here Comes Santa Claus." The inspiration for the song came from Autry's time as a grand marshal for the 1946 Christmas parade in Hollywood, which took place on the seasonally renamed Santa Claus Lane.

When St. Nick closed out the parade, Autry could hear kids yelling, "Here comes Santa Claus! Here comes Santa Claus!"—which inspired the bridge for Autry's famous song. Elvis' version is notably more bouncy and playful, though he prefers the pronunciation "Santa Claus" over Autry's western drawl of "Sant-y Claus."

The song has been covered by many other artists, including the Beach Boys (1974), Willie Nelson (1979), RuPaul (1997), Bob Dylan (2009), and perhaps most memorably, Alvin and the Chipmunks (1961).

"I'll Be Home for Christmas"

WRITTEN BY KIM GANNON AND WALTER KENT;
BUCK RAM LATER RECEIVED A COWRITING CREDIT | RECORDED SEPTEMBER 7, 1957

This wartime Christmas standard would take on new significance for Presley, who, 104 days after recording the song, would get drafted into military service. Presley was again wading into the territory of Bing Crosby, who made this song a classic in 1943. The song recounts the story of a soldier stationed overseas who pines for snow and Christmas traditions. The soldier's declaration that "you can plan on me" coming home is tempered by the melancholy refrain "I'll be home for Christmas, if only in my dreams."

The song cast a shadow over Presley's own military career, during which he longed for his home and his mother, Gladys Presley, who died eight months after his service began. Presley was given an emergency leave from basic training at Fort Hood to see his ailing mother, who died of a heart attack at age forty-six.

"She was all we lived for," Elvis told the press. "It broke my heart. She was always my best girl."

After the funeral, Presley traveled to Germany, and for the next eighteen months he rose through the ranks from private to sergeant in Company D's 32nd Tank Battalion in the 3rd Armored Division. During his time in Germany, Presley met fourteen-year-old Priscilla Beaulieu, whose military family was stationed in Germany. He would marry her eight years later.

IN 1958, AFTER HIS MOTHER DIED, ELVIS WAS IN GERMANY DURING THE holidays—when he missed Gladys most.

One day around Christmas, as the soldier prepared for holiday leave, one of his fellow soldiers began singing Christmas songs, accompanying himself on a guitar. After a subdued Elvis joined the gathering of the other soldiers in a sing-along, he began singing "Silent Night" and the room went quiet.

"Those going on pass didn't interrupt. They simply walked silently by Elvis, touched his shoulder, and walked out the door. Not another word was spoken after the song until Elvis broke the spell," Reconnaissance Platoon Sergeant Ira Jones told Peter Guralnick for his book *Careless Love*.

Elvis sang "as if in a trance, totally oblivious" to his surroundings, Jones said.

Elvis then wished everyone a Merry Christmas and departed for the Hotel Grunewald with his father, where they were celebrating the holidays.

"Blue Christmas"

WRITTEN BY BILLY HAYES AND JAY JOHNSON | RECORDED SEPTEMBER 5, 1957

Elvis may have been treading on Bing Crosby's turf with "White Christmas," but he made "Blue Christmas" very much his own. The song had originally been recorded by Western actor Doye O'Dell and a few other artists, but was transformed into a bona fide country hit by the Texas Troubadour, Ernest Tubb, in 1950. Presley dropped the fiddles and steel guitar twang and embraced the bluesy, ethereal "woo-wee-woo" of his backing vocalist, Millie Kirkham, on this moody 1957 version.

Kirkham was known as Nashville's "on-call soprano" and Elvis had admired her vocals on Ferlin Husky's "Gone." She was six months pregnant when she arrived in the studio for the recording session. "Someone get this woman a chair!" Elvis said.

According to Kirkham, Elvis did not want to record "Blue Christmas," but had been told it was already on the schedule. He'd already recorded fifteen takes of "Treat Me Nice" and had abandoned "My Wish Came True" after several hours of trying to get it right. A tired Elvis wasn't feeling particularly festive about "Blue Christmas."

"He didn't want to do it," Kirkham remembered in a 2012 Country Music Hall of Fame interview, but Elvis finally relented.

"Let's just get this over with," Elvis said, turning to his backing singers and band. "Do anything. Have fun. Do something silly."

So that's what Kirkham did. When she started singing her "woo-wee-woo"

backing vocals, Elvis motioned for her to continue and she sang it for the duration of the song.

"When we got through it, we all laughed and said, 'Well, that's one record that the record company will never release,'" Kirkham remembered.

But RCA did release it. "Blue Christmas" became a decades-spanning hit and Elvis' signature Christmas song. Kirkham's improvisational backup vocals became as inseparable from the song as Aretha Franklin's sisters singing "sock it to me" behind her enduring hit "Respect."

Kirkham jokes that her daughter Shelly, still in utero, was there at her first session with Elvis. "Maybe I was kicking you," her daughter told her mother. "Maybe that's the reason you were going woo-wee-ooo!"

Later, Elvis performed "Blue Christmas" on NBC, in what became known as the *'68 Comeback Special.*

In the special, Elvis introduces the song by saying, "I'd like to do my favorite Christmas song of the ones I've recorded."

However, this quote was edited into the show from a different take. He actually said this before recording "Santa Claus Is Back in Town"—a favorite by songwriters Jerry Leiber and Mike Stoller. That song didn't make the cut for the show because he couldn't quite remember the words and abandoned the song midway through the recording.

The show contains some of the only footage of Elvis ever performing Christmas songs, aside from a rehearsal snippet of "Santa Claus Is Back in Town" from special editions of the 1970 documentary *Elvis: That's the Way It Is*, directed by Denis Sanders.

EACH YEAR, ELVIS DONATED MORE THAN $50,000 TO LOCAL MEMPHIS CHARITIES. A few days before Christmas, his friend Jerry Schilling remembered, Elvis would "sit in the living room with his father and go through a list of fifty local Memphis charities he'd asked the city to provide for him. . . . Every year, each of the charities on the list got a thousand-dollar check from Elvis. Some celebrities might have made a big PR moment out of that kind of giving, but for Elvis it was private and personal, part of the holiday season in his home."

Elvis spontaneously donated to charities no matter the time of year. Known recipients included the NAACP, the Jaycees, Memphis Hebrew Academy, the YMCA, and St. Jude Children's Research Hospital.

"Never doubt my love for you, always trust
me and believe me when I say that I love you.
It sure is going to be a blue Christmas this year.
But in 15 short months it'll be over and as
General MacArthur said, 'I shall return.' Have a
Merry Christmas Darling and rem[em]ber there
is a lonely little boy 5,000 miles away that is
counting the hour till he returns to your arms."

(ELVIS IN A LETTER WRITTEN FROM GERMANY TO HIS
GIRLFRIEND ANITA WOOD, POSTMARKED NOVEMBER 14, 1958)

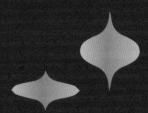

"Santa Bring My Baby Back (To Me)"

WRITTEN BY AARON SCHROEDER AND CLAUDE DEMETRIUS | RECORDED SEPTEMBER 7, 1957

Playful and springy (and perhaps a little too close to his hit "Teddy Bear"), Elvis whips his way through this pop number with support from his favorite backing group, the Jordanaires.

He declares:

The Christmas tree is ready
The candles all aglow
But with my baby far away
What good is mistletoe?

Songwriter Aaron Schroeder penned seventeen songs for Elvis, including "Stuck on You," "It's Now or Never," and "A Big Hunk o' Love."

"He was probably the artist that I worked the hardest to write for," said Schroeder. "He was a combination of many styles—rhythm and blues, country, pop. . . . He embodied that blending that is oh so American. It was difficult to write something for him because I had to put a little bit of this and a little bit of that into each song. The lyrics would always take a long time. . . . He was and is a legend."

"He had a unique, identifiable quality in his voice. And that's what makes the stars and legends," Schroeder added. "When you turn on the radio and you know without question who it is that's singing. And he had that. He sang from his soul."

"O Little Town of Bethlehem"

WRITTEN BY PHILLIPS BROOKS AND LEWIS REDNER,
ARRANGEMENT BY ELVIS PRESLEY | RECORDED SEPTEMBER 7, 1957

Side two of 1957's *Elvis' Christmas Album* struck a more traditional tone, embracing Presley's love of gospel music and church hymns. He started with a solemn version of "O Little Town of Bethlehem," banishing Santa to the back seat and letting Jesus take the wheel.

Not everyone was a fan of the change in tone, however, or the commingling of religious and pop music.

Sheila Whiteley puts it succinctly in her 2008 book, *Christmas, Ideology and Popular Culture*. By moving "O Little Town of Bethlehem" into the realm of pop music, Whiteley wrote, "the message is taken into a secular context. In effect, the alignment of a carol describing the quiet beauty of Christ's birthplace with a song situating Christmas within a nostalgic winter landscape effects a shared romantic discourse, which is heightened by Presley's mellow crooning baritone."

"The inclusion of a prayer to Santa to return his 'baby' adds myth to the vernacular of a pop love song and, as such, it is not difficult to see why the Bible belt attacked the album as amoral, profaning both Christmas and Christianity."

In just four takes, however, Elvis captured the hushed grace of Phillips Brooks and Lewis Redner's original composition, written in 1865 after the chaos of the Civil War.

Brooks had found some acclaim for his eulogy of slain president Abraham Lincoln in Philadelphia, but he was still finding his spiritual footing as a clergyman. Seeking solace and spiritual recharging, the young Episcopal priest went on a Christmas pilgrimage to Jerusalem, only to find it crowded with other truth seekers. So, on Christmas Eve, he set out on a borrowed horse by himself and rode into Bethlehem, then still a remote village. Being there, in those modest surroundings, filled Brooks with a "singing in [his] soul" as he contemplated the first Christmas.

In his journal, Brooks wrote: "Before dark we rode out of town to the field where they say the shepherds saw the star. It is a fenced piece of ground with a cave in it, in which, strangely enough, they put the shepherds. . . . Somewhere in those fields we rode through, the shepherds must have been. As we passed, the shepherds were still 'keeping watch over their flocks,' or leading them home . . ."

It took Brooks another three years to shape the experience into a poem, after which organist Redner shaped it into a song. Later in life, Brooks would become a mentor to Helen Keller and his sermons would be collected into a best-selling book, although he'll always be best known for "O Little Town of Bethlehem," one of the most celebrated Christmas carols in history.

ELVIS' CHRISTMAS RITUALS

IN THE 1960S, AFTER MEMBERS OF ELVIS' ENTOURAGE LEFT GRACELAND LATE on Christmas Eve, Elvis would go for a drive late at night with Priscilla and another couple. "Elvis loved seeing what everybody else's Christmas decorations looked like," remembered friend George Klein.

"Silent Night"

WRITTEN BY JOSEPH MOHR AND FRANZ GRUBER | RECORDED SEPTEMBER 6, 1957

Elvis was back in Bing Crosby territory again with "Silent Night." Although the song was written in 1818, Crosby's 1935 recording made it the fourth-best-selling single of all time (ahead of Bill Haley & His Comets' "Rock around the Clock" and Whitney Houston's cover of "I Will Always Love You," but behind Mungo Jerry's "In the Summertime"). What is the number-one best-selling single of all time? Crosby's rendition of "White Christmas."

For some critics, Elvis' covers of Christmas standards amounted to musical sacrilege. Associated Press writer Hugh Mulligan dubbed the album "a masterpiece of seasonal miscasting." It seemed that this critic could not separate the pop star from the pilgrim.

Adding insult to injury, the reviewer wrote: "Most of the time, he's so hushfully reverent in his approach to these unfamiliar themes that he just isn't there at all."

Time has proven otherwise, however. Elvis' rendition of "Silent Night," with soaring vocals and a respectful arrangement, made a sacred song popular with mainstream music lovers.

"We had a Christmas party here.
I had a lot of guys from over at the post,
you know. I had many of the boys here as
possible at my home . . . to kind of make
them feel at home around Christmastime.
And we had a little Christmas party and on
New Year's we had another little party and it
seemed nice. It was better than last year!"

(ELVIS IN CONVERSATION WITH
DISC JOCKEY DICK CLARK WHILE ELVIS WAS
IN THE ARMY IN GERMANY, 1960)

"(There'll Be) Peace in the Valley (For Me)"

WRITTEN BY THOMAS A. DORSEY | RECORDED JANUARY 13, 1957

This gospel hymn was a favorite song of Elvis', and a repositioning of his brand. Presley first performed "(There'll Be) Peace in the Valley (For Me)" on *The Ed Sullivan Show* on January 6, 1957, his third appearance on the show and a cultural triumph. Originally, Sullivan had been dismissive of Elvis, sniffing, "He is not my cup of tea."

However, after ratings for Presley's appearance on *The Steve Allen Show* trounced Sullivan's, he could no longer ignore the cultural phenomenon from Tupelo, Mississippi. Soon after, *The Ed Sullivan Show* paid Elvis the unheard-of sum of $50,000 for three appearances in late 1956 and early 1957.

On this third night—after performing hits including "Heartbreak Hotel," "Love Me Tender," "Too Much," and "Hound Dog"—Elvis struck a solemn chord. Surrounded by the Jordanaires, Presley launched into "(There'll Be) Peace in the Valley (For Me)." This spiritual standard showed audiences that he was more than lips and hips, that he was also spirit and soul. The performance is mostly a straight gospel rendition, although he Elvis'ed it up by turning the word "for" into a four-syllable word and transforming his "whoa-oh-oh yes" into a rockabilly "hallelujah."

After the performance, Sullivan declared: "I wanted to say to Elvis Presley and the country that this is a real decent, fine boy, and wherever you go, Elvis, all of you . . . we want to say that we've never had a pleasanter experience on our show with a big name than we've had with you. So now let's have a tremendous hand for a very nice person."

Seven days later, Elvis recorded the song as the title track for his EP *Peace in the Valley*. The cover, featuring Elvis in a suit jacket—and (*gasp!*) even a tie—was meant to reassure parents that under the bravado and swagger was a clean-cut, churchgoing young man. In the photo, he might even be mistaken for someone their daughter could meet at choir practice.

It's worth noting that the song has World War II roots, as described by song-writer Thomas A. Dorsey:

> "Just before Hitler sent his war chariots into Western Europe, I was on a train going through southern Indiana on the way to Cincinnati, and the country seemed upset about this coming war. . . . I passed through a valley on the train. Horses, cows, and sheep were all grazing together in this little valley. A little brook was running through the valley, and up the hill I could see where the water was falling from. Everything seemed so peaceful with all the animals down there grazing together. It made me wonder what's the matter with humanity? What's the matter with man-kind? Why couldn't man live in peace like the animals down there?"

Dorsey began scribbling the words to his song, taking inspiration from the spiritual standard "Walk through the Valley of Peace" and the Old Testament.

In Isaiah 11:6, the prophet describes Christ's peaceful rule over Earth:

The wolf shall dwell with the lamb,

And the leopard shall lie down with the kid;

And the calf and the young lion and the fatling together;

And a little child shall lead them.

Elvis loved the song. During the sessions, he said, "It's easy. I could sing this song all day. . . . I can put some blues in there."

Other songs on the *Peace in the Valley* EP—"It Is No Secret (What God Can Do)," "I Believe," and "Take My Hand, Precious Lord"—were included on *Elvis' Christmas Album* to round out side two of the album.

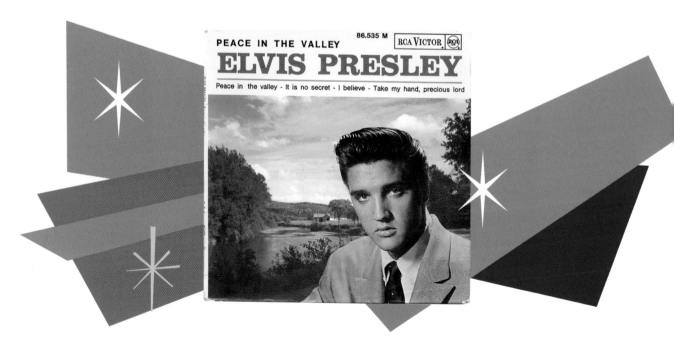

IT WAS OVER AN EXTENDED CHRISTMAS BREAK IN 1956 THAT ELVIS STOPPED BY SUN STUDIO, where he had cut his first records with Sam Phillips. During that visit, on December 4, Elvis encountered Carl Perkins recording with his brothers and a then unknown piano player named Jerry Lee Lewis. The spur-of-the-moment jam session turned into something more when Phillips called Johnny Cash, who arrived shortly after. How long he remained, and if you can hear him on the recording, has been much debated.

Cash wrote in his autobiography, "Contrary to what some people have written, my voice is on the tape. It's not obvious, because I was farthest away from the mic and I was singing a lot higher than I usually did in order to stay in key with Elvis, but I guarantee you, I'm there."

Together, they recorded more than forty tracks, in part or in whole, including "Down by the Riverside," "Don't Be Cruel," and instrumental versions of "Jingle Bells" and "White Christmas."

Bob Johnson, the *Memphis Press-Scimitar*'s entertainment editor, visited the studio and wrote an article about the session. The headline read: "Million Dollar Quartet."

The recordings were released years later and Elvis' visit to Sun Studio became immortalized in the 2006 jukebox musical also called *Million Dollar Quartet*.

"I Believe"

WRITTEN BY ERVIN DRAKE, IRVIN GRAHAM,
JIMMY SHIRL, AND AL STILLMAN | RECORDED JANUARY 12, 1957

Recording artist Frankie Laine, who first made a hit of "I Believe" in 1953, said this of the song: "The lyrics were a simple, but moving declaration of faith, and seldom had words touched me so deeply. It was almost more of a prayer than a song."

Ervin Drake, a Tin Pan Alley songwriter, wrote this spiritual standard and a host of other songs, including, "Good Morning Heartache" and "It Was a Very Good Year."

For Elvis, the love of gospel was sincere.

"Lots of people make fun of what they call 'Holy Rollers.' They look on them as ignorant and not really religious at all," Elvis told one reporter. "In the church we belong to, we really feel our religion and get carried away with it. I think spirituals are the best songs in the world; they got a beat and folks down our way really feel that music. Someday I'm gonna record me some spirituals."

Elvis was true to his word, producing several gospel records—the source of his only Grammy wins. After he recorded "I Believe," the song was covered by Louis Armstrong and—much later—Barbra Streisand and LeAnn Rimes.

OVER ELVIS' CAREER, DOZENS OF NOVELTY SONGS WERE RECORDED BY OTHER ARTISTS about him—and at least fifteen of them were Christmas-themed.

Some of them were covers; others were variations on a theme. In 1960 Bobbie Jean crooned, "I Don't Want a Bunny or Dolly (I Just Want Elvis Instead)," and two years later Mary Kaye recorded "I Don't Want a Bracelet or Diamond, I Just Want Elvis Instead." Each song featured a young teenage girl who promises to do her chores, if only she'd find Elvis under the Christmas tree this year.

One song, written by Don Kirshner and Bobby Darin, got four different titles and releases in 1956 at the height of Elvis mania:

"I Wanna Spend Christmas with Elvis" recorded by Marlene Paula

"I Wanna Spend Xmas with Elvis" recorded by Little "Lambsie" Penn

"I Want to Spend Christmas with Elvis" recorded by Debbie Dabney (which was really just a reissue of the Marlene Paula recording under a different name)

"I Want Elvis for Christmas" recorded by the Holly Twins (with Eddie Cochran doing an Elvis impression)

That song went, in part:

You ain't nothing but a reindeer, prancin' all the time

Well if you ain't here for Christmas

Then you ain't no friend of mine

So Elvis, spend Christmas with me

And, if you can find it, 1957's "Elvis for Christmas" by Mad Milo—a pastiche of DJ chatter, audio clips, and impressions—is worth a listen.

"Take My Hand, Precious Lord"

(FROM *PEACE IN THE VALLEY*, 1957)

WRITTEN BY THOMAS A. DORSEY | RECORDED JANUARY 13, 1957

This is the second of two Thomas A. Dorsey songs Elvis recorded, after "(There'll Be) Peace in the Valley (For Me)."

Dorsey was in a particularly dark place when he wrote "Take My Hand, Precious Lord," having lost both his wife and baby during a difficult delivery. For days, Dorsey drove Chicago's streets, lost in mourning, while the beginning of a song began to form in his head. After a few days spent despairing, Dorsey visited Theodore Frye, a gospel singer and friend. And in the basement of a former hairdressing school, Dorsey began to compose "Take My Hand, Precious Lord."

"The next Sunday morning Frye's choir sang it at the Ebenezer Baptist Church and I played the accompaniment," Dorsey remembered. "It tore up the church."

The Georgia-born Dorsey was a Black songwriter who was steeped in gospel music and Chicago-style blues music. He wrote the ragtime hit "It's Tight Like That" under the name Georgia Tom with collaborator Tampa Red.

Like Elvis, Dorsey was a musical trailblazer, whose innovative combining of different genres was controversial with some audiences—especially churchgoers who didn't like the blues mixed in with their traditional worship music.

"I got thrown out of some of the best churches in those days," Dorsey said, which made him the perfect songwriter for Elvis.

"Take My Hand, Precious Lord" was a favorite of Dr. Martin Luther King Jr., and Mahalia Jackson sang it at the civil rights leader's funeral in 1968. It was likewise sung at the funeral of President Lyndon B. Johnson by opera singer Leontyne Price. Other artists who recorded the song include Roy Rogers, B. B. King, Tennessee Ernie Ford, and Aretha Franklin. In 2015, Beyoncé brought the song into the twenty-first century with her performance of "Take My Hand, Precious Lord" at the 57th Annual Grammy Awards.

Dorsey was forever a champion of crossover music and wrote more than 250 gospel songs. "I write all my songs with a message," Dorsey said. "All people are my people. . . . I try to lift their spirits and let them know that God still loves them. I want them to understand that God is still in business and he's still saving and he can give them power."

"It Is No Secret (What God Can Do)"

(FROM *PEACE IN THE VALLEY*, 1957)
WRITTEN BY STUART HAMBLEN | RECORDED JANUARY 19, 1957

The origin story of this modern hymn features a cameo from John Wayne.

Stuart Hamblen was a singing cowboy and jack-of-all trades in 1949, a radio host of note as well as an actor (in 1946's *King of the Forest Rangers*) and a writer of country songs. Hamblen also developed a reputation for his love of booze and women, although both brought him trouble. When a tent revival preacher invited Hamblen to get saved, the disc jockey reformed his ways, although it cost him his job when he refused to promote a beer company on the air.

"It's No Secret" has a colorful origin story. In one version of the tale, a friend named John asks Hamblen about his abrupt conversion. In another version, it's not just *a* John, it's John *Wayne*, who crosses paths with Hamblen on Hollywood Boulevard.

"Hey, I heard what happened to you," Wayne said.

"I guess it's no secret," Hamblen replied.

"That sounds like a song to me!" said Wayne.

By the end of that night, it was. In 1950, "It Is No Secret (What God Can Do)" was a surprise crossover hit, appearing on both the Top 40 pop chart and rising to number three on the country-and-western chart.

Hamblen penned a few more popular songs, including "His Hands," "Open Up Your Heart and Let the Sun Shine In," and "This Ole House," which Rosemary Clooney made a number-one hit in 1955.

"It Is No Secret (What God Can Do)" has also endured, with versions recorded by both Mahalia Jackson and Johnny Cash. Elvis included it as the last song on his religious EP *Peace in the Valley.*

IN 1964, ELVIS' FRIENDS—LED BY MARTY LACKER—PRESENTED HIM WITH A special, leather-bound Bible with a design of the tree of life, based on a sketch by Lacker, printed on its first page.

"Elvis' name was on the trunk of the tree and each of the guys got their own branch," remembered friend Jerry Schilling. "Written below the tree in English, Latin, and Hebrew was one of Elvis' favorite quotations, 'And ye shall know the truth, and the truth shall set you free.'"

"On holidays, I miss her the most. At Graceland we make the most of Christmas. So far I've had the good luck to be sure I am always home for Christmas. That has always been a rule!"

(ELVIS SPEAKING OF HIS MOTHER, 1965)

ELVIS LOVED CHRISTMAS LIGHTS, AND AT GRACELAND HOLIDAY decorations went up early and came down late, usually remaining until Elvis' birthday on January 8. It's still a tradition at Graceland. During Elvis' first year at Graceland, which he purchased in 1957, he wanted to go big. So, on December 12, he paid the Bain Sign Company $300 for a yard display featuring Santa and his reindeer, along with the message "Merry Christmas to All, Elvis."

The display went missing for half a century, until it was found by staff in one of the Graceland stables. Those same decorations, now restored, are used today.

BONUS TRACK
"If Every Day Was Like Christmas"

WRITTEN BY RED WEST | RECORDED JUNE 11–12, 1966

Robert Gene "Red" West, Elvis' longtime friend and a member of his Memphis Mafia entourage, wrote "If Every Day Was Like Christmas" in less than ninety minutes. One August night in 1965, Elvis had rented the Memphian movie theater for himself and his friends. And it was there, West remembered, that "the urge . . . to write a holiday song" hit him. He recalled, "I got home, didn't say anything to anybody and wrote 'If Every Day Was Like Christmas.'"

Red West had originally recorded the single himself under the name Bobby West and put it out on his own Memphis label in 1965—but to little acclaim. About two thousand copies were pressed on the Brent label, named after West's son.

The song remains an outlier in the King of Rock 'n' Roll's Christmas catalog, because it appeared as a single off his 1966 gospel album *How Great Thou Art*—an album otherwise devoid of holiday songs.

The recording of the song came from a troubled session, during which Elvis wasn't even in the studio. Although the official reason was a throat infection, music scholar Ernst Jorgensen was unconvinced: "Maybe his throat was sore; perhaps he resented being forced into the studio again. There was no way to be sure." This was a period in Elvis' career when subpar movie soundtracks (see *Harum Scarum* and *Spinout*) had dominated his session time, and there was a struggle between Elvis, the Colonel, and his producers over what material might produce a radio hit.

So that left West to sing in Presley's absence in RCA's Studio B in Nashville in June of 1966. With a full band in attendance, including Elvis' go-to musicians—guitarist Scotty Moore, drummer D. J. Fontana, and backing vocalists the Jordanaires—West provided the guide tracks on three songs: "Indescribably Blue," "I'll Remember You," and "If Every Day Was Like Christmas."

The next day, West took the tracks to Elvis' hotel room, along with a two-track tape recorder.

"Elvis wanted to hear it . . . and right there in the hotel he put his voice over it. He loved the songs," West remembered. On June 12, Elvis returned to the studio and professionally recorded all three songs in less than thirty minutes.

Afterward, Elvis wrote an uncharacteristic thank-you note to Felton Jarvis, RCA's producer:

"Please convey how much I deeply appreciate the cooperation and consideration shown to me and my associates during my last two trips to Nashville. I would like to thank you, the engineers, musicians, singers, and everyone connected with the sessions. Please see that every one of them know my feelings. And as General McArthur [sic] once said, 'I shall return.'"

Although "If Every Day Was Like Christmas" originally appeared on *How Great Thou Art*, the single has since been added to numerous Christmas collections, including reissues of *Elvis' Christmas Album* (1970, 1975, 1985), and lent its title to the *If Every Day Was Like Christmas* release in 1994.

"HOW GREAT THOU ART"—THE SONG—WOULD BE ONE OF ONLY TWO SONGS FOR WHICH ELVIS ever received Grammys. Despite his undeniable impact on music (U2's Bono called him the "Big Bang of Rock 'n' Roll"), Presley was awarded only three Grammys in his lifetime. All were for gospel songs. For 1972's "He Touched Me," Elvis won a Best Inspirational Performance Grammy. "How Great Thou Art" won Elvis two golden gramophones, seven years apart. In 1967 he was awarded a Grammy for Best Sacred Performance for "How Great Thou Art," and in 1974 he received a Grammy for Best Inspirational Performance (Non-classical) for his soulful rendition of the song on his album *Recorded Live on Stage in Memphis*.

Three Grammys for a career of record-breaking hits seems like an injustice. After all, 50,000 Elvis fans can't be wrong.

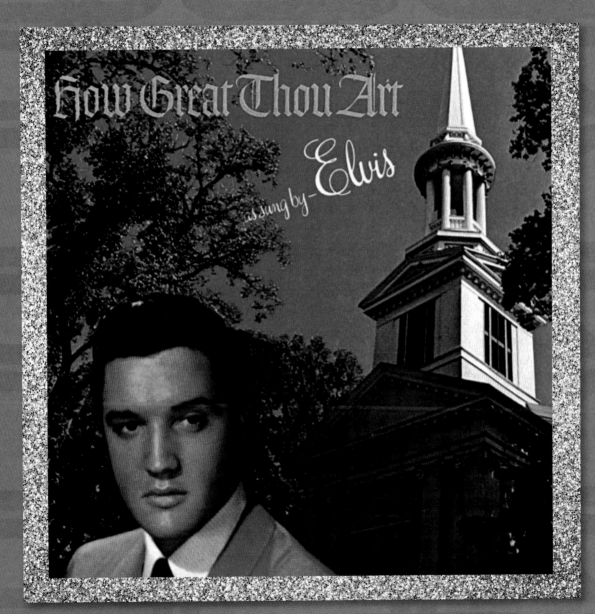

How Great Thou Art

Elvis

as sung by-

THE '68 COMEBACK SPECIAL

ELVIS ON THE AIR, IN LEATHER, IN DECEMBER

PERHAPS ELVIS' BIGGEST CHRISTMAS GIFT TO HIS FANS ISN'T remembered as a Christmas gift at all—and for good reason.

In 1968, Colonel Tom Parker envisioned a Chrismas special for Elvis, which would be his first televised appearance since 1960. It was a strange time for Elvis, then thirty-three, who was no longer the King of Rock 'n' Roll in the eyes of the public. He'd been eclipsed by the Beatles—who had just released their double "White" album—and Jim Morrison and Mick Jagger were pop music's sex symbols of the day.

Parker cut a deal with NBC for Elvis to sing Christmas carols in front of a live audience, as a way to reintroduce him to the public. In the 1960s, variety show specials were holiday staples, regularly hosted by Bob Hope, Perry Como, and Andy Williams. Even Judy Garland got her own Christmas broadcast in 1963. But it wasn't the kind of company Elvis, who was already worried about his cultural relevance, wanted to keep.

What made it worse? The special, titled *Singer Presents . . . Elvis*, would be sponsored by the Singer Company, best known for its sewing machines—not exactly the hippest sponsor.

What did Elvis "want to stand up and sing a bunch of Christmas carols on national TV for?" wrote biographer Peter Guralnick. "He felt angry and frustrated, he felt like the Colonel was turning him into a joke."

Enter Steve Binder, a young producer/director with impressive television credits and the theatrical concert movie *The T.A.M.I. Show* under his belt. Using his crew from *The Steve Allen Show*, Binder shot acts such as the Rolling Stones, James Brown, the Supremes, the Beach Boys, and others with handheld equipment for *The T.A.M.I. Show*, giving the performances a more "live" and spontaneous feel.

Binder sold Elvis on the idea that the special wouldn't be a hokey holiday show. It would not be "a lot of songs strung together with pretty scenery and colorful costumes, but a subliminal tale of his personal life journey," Binder wrote. "At the end of the day, viewers would really feel they knew him as a compassionate and loving person as well as a great singer and entertainer."

This sounded great—to everyone but the Colonel. Parker insisted on Christmas themes and songs, which set off a behind-the-scenes fight for creative control. Eventually, the Colonel backed off, but insisted that there be at least one Christmas song on the show.

"I don't think the Colonel really cared whether the special was a Christmas show or not, or if there was even one Christmas song in it," Binder wrote years later. "All he wanted was to keep his power over Elvis in front of people who he considered 'outsiders'—like me."

But Binder ultimately persevered over the Colonel's demands. Hit songs were updated with more orchestration, and new numbers such as the raucous "Trouble" and the soaring "If I Can Dream" were added. Binder produced two sets with Elvis' old bandmates—guitarist Scotty Moore and drummer D.J. Fontana—adding the talents of guitarists Alan Fortas and Charlie Hodge, in a sit-down set that created a sense of intimacy and immediacy.

"We were working with an artist who was rediscovering himself and loving the hell out of it!" Binder remembered in his book *Comeback '68 | Elvis: The Story of the Elvis Special*.

Despite some day-of jitters (Elvis' mind went blank and he didn't want to go out on stage), the show was an absolute triumph.

"It was the finest music of his life. If ever there was music that bleeds, this was it," wrote biographer and critic Greil Marcus in his 1975 book, *Mystery Train*.

The show, which debuted December 3, 1968, is remembered as the '68 Comeback Special. It injected new life into Elvis' recording career and led him back to the stage. It was a full-on career resurgence.

"It really is the best season of the year. The Christmas carols, trees, and lights just grab you. There's something about Christmas and being home that I just can't explain. Maybe it's being with family and with friends, time to read and to study."

(ELVIS IN A HOLIDAY INTERVIEW WITH THE *MEMPHIS PRESS-SCIMITAR*, 1966)

Ultimately, and after all the squabbling with Binder, the Colonel got his way. Both "Blue Christmas" and "Santa Claus Is Back in Town" were recorded for the show, although only "Blue Christmas" made it into the final cut. This "Blue Christmas" was raw and fun and Elvis' friend Hodge can be heard urging him to "play it dirty, play it dirty," to make it an earthier, freewheeling performance.

In an August 1969 rebroadcast of the show, "Blue Christmas" was replaced with "Tiger Man," which was more fitting for a summer airing. Both "Blue Christmas" and "Santa Claus Is Back in Town" were later added to deluxe editions of *Elvis: '68 Comeback Special*.

STEVE BINDER, IN ADDITION TO PRODUCING ARGUABLY THE BEST TV MUSIC specials of all time with Elvis, also created one of the most infamous: the 1978 *Star Wars Holiday Special*. That, however, is another book entirely. The two-hour CBS special featured original *Star Wars* cast members Mark Hamill, Harrison Ford, and Carrie Fisher, as well as TV comedians Bea Arthur and Harvey Korman in genre-crossing segments that bombed. At least we got Boba Fett, who made his debut in a ten-minute animated special, out of the deal. Elvis had passed on by the time the *Star Wars* special aired, although he would have undoubtedly improved it as a leather-clad, rakish bounty hunter.

ELVIS SINGS THE ✳ WONDERFUL WORLD OF CHRISTMAS, SONG BY SONG

ELVIS
sings
The Wonderful World of Christmas

Winter Wonderland

If I Get Home on Christmas Day

It Won't Seem Like Christmas (Without You)

The First Noel

I'll Be Home on Christmas Day

Silver Bells

Holly Leaves and Christmas Trees

O Come, All Ye Faithful

On a Snowy Christmas Night

On a Snowy Christmas Night

The Wonderful World of Christmas

Merry Christmas Baby

ELVIS SINGS THE WONDERFUL WORLD OF CHRISTMAS (October 1971)

O ddly enough, Elvis' second Christmas album doesn't appear to feature Elvis on the cover at all. But if you squint, you can see black-and-white photos of Elvis' face pasted over both Santa's tiny, cheery visage and a snowman in the lower left corner.

This was the beginning of Elvis' Vegas phase, when his collars were almost as big as his opulent stage show.

"The collars keep the draft off my neck and the capes make me feel like Superman," Elvis said.

Elvis Sings the Wonderful World of Christmas, recorded in May of 1971, was a return to the holiday market.

RCA's Studio B in Nashville was decorated with a Christmas tree and piles of brightly colored presents (mostly empty boxes). Lamar Fike, Elvis' longtime friend and the head of his publishing company in Nashville, even dressed up as Santa. The session was part of a weeklong recording binge, featuring a mix of holiday classics ("Silver Bells" and "The First Noel") and new songs, including "Holly Leaves and Christmas Trees" and "It Won't Seem Like Christmas (Without You)."

Chris Arnold, a songwriter and member of the British pop band Butterscotch, was present for at least one night of the session. Arnold had cowritten several songs recorded by Presley, including "Let's Be Friends," "This Is the Story," and "A Little Bit of Green."

"This was to be a Christmas album, and down there in Nashville it was the middle of May and about 85 degrees and very un-Christmas like," Arnold told the British music newspaper *Disc* in 1971. "But obviously Elvis had thought about this and had arranged for a great big decorated Christmas tree to be brought into the studio. There were also presents for all: Elvis, close associates, and musicians. They received gold bracelets engraved 'Elvis 1971.'"

Arnold described Elvis walking into the studio: "He's tall, about 6 foot 2 inches, but he seems even bigger because he has a kind of presence about him which dominates the whole room. But even so, the musicians just treat him as another Nashville boy; another Tennessee musician, like themselves. Okay, so he's made it big, but they still feel very much on the same level as him, and that was one of the nicest things about the session; the very easy relationship between everyone. They all call him El or E."

Arnold was taken by the "live" nature of the recording session, with Elvis on a microphone and the musicians gathered around him in a semicircle.

"Another thing that impressed me was the tireless devotion to getting it absolutely right. They would go over and over the song, getting a better feel. Each time it built up a little more. The guitarist would put in an extra little riff, or there would be an extra fill from the piano, and Elvis would acknowledge it every time anyone did something like that," Arnold said.

But Presley wasn't always "at home" in the material, Arnold observed. "He was putting his heart into the singing but after a couple of numbers everybody was sort of chafing at the bit, and wanting to get into something really go-ey [up-tempo]."

One of those "go-ey" numbers included an off-the-cuff, up-tempo rendition of "Don't Think Twice, It's All Right." Guitarist James Burton kicked off a jam around Bob Dylan's classic that lasted more than eleven minutes. (The Dylan cover was cut down to 2:45 on its initial 1973 release, although other versions do exist, including a more expansive 8:36 version on *Our Memories of Elvis Vol. 2* in 1979). After Elvis finished up the Christmas songs, he also recorded a recent favorite, Kris Kristofferson's "Help Me Make It Through the Night," on the third night of the sessions (released on 1972's *Elvis Now*).

Reviews were generally encouraging. Canada's *Star-Phoenix* newspaper wrote that Elvis "put the beat into Christmas with 'Merry Christmas Baby,' a 5:45 bluesy romp, with good blues piano in the background. Other selections aren't as familiar but are ballad-type melodies, all extolling the wonders and values of Christmas and the values of being home."

A *Billboard* reviewer wrote of *Elvis Sings the Wonderful World of Christmas*, "Elvis offers some of the best standards of the holiday season in this package which should prove a giant seller." The album, released in October 1971, hit number two on *Billboard*'s Christmas album chart—but also went to number one on the same chart in 1972 and 1973.

TRACK LIST

ELVIS SINGS THE WONDERFUL WORLD OF CHRISTMAS

SIDE 1

1. "O Come, All Ye Faithful"
2. "The First Noel"
3. "On a Snowy Christmas Night"
4. "Winter Wonderland"
5. "The Wonderful World of Christmas"
6. "It Won't Seem Like Christmas (Without You)"

SIDE 2

1. "I'll Be Home on Christmas Day"
2. "If I Get Home On Christmas Day"
3. "Holly Leaves and Christmas Trees"
4. "Merry Christmas Baby"
5. "Silver Bells"

"O Come, All Ye Faithful"

ENGLISH VERSION WRITTEN BY FREDERICK OAKELEY,
ORIGINAL LATIN HYMN "ADESTE FIDELES"
CREDITED TO JOHN FRANCIS WADE | RECORDED MAY 16, 1971

Unlike Elvis' first Christmas album, which started with rock and ended with reverence, his second outing begins squarely in the church pew with "O Come, All Ye Faithful."

Frederick Oakeley (1802–1880) was ordained by the Church of England in 1828, although he converted to Catholicism in 1841. His translation of John Francis Wade's Latin hymn "Adeste Fideles" originally began with the line "Ye faithful, approach ye"—which, let's all agree, doesn't exactly roll off the tongue. After his conversion, Oakeley reworked the hymn, including the opening line "O come, all ye faithful, joyful and triumphant."

Backed by a choir, Elvis delivers the line in a deep baritone, belting it out in later verses like an opera singer, leaning into the vibrato.

ELVIS CHRISTMAS TALES

ON CHRISTMAS EVE 1970, ELVIS AND HIS ENTOURAGE VISITED THE SHELBY COUNTY JAIL IN MEMPHIS. When a confused sergeant on duty asked what Elvis was doing there, Elvis replied, "Nothing else is open on Christmas Eve, so we thought we'd come visit you guys."

After chatting with officers on duty, he asked for permission to visit the men in the cell block. There, Elvis shook hands with prisoners and entertained them with an impromptu rendition of "White Christmas," remembered his friend George Klein.

The prisoners asked him: "Elvis, can I have a Cadillac?" and "Elvis, will you be my lawyer?"

Elvis spotted a familiar face behind bars: Harold Poole, who had been several years ahead of Elvis in high school.

"Aw, Harold," Elvis said. "What are you doing here?"

"Well, I got in a little barroom fight, Elvis, that's all," Poole said.

Elvis ended up posting bail for Poole and returned to his cell.

"You're settled up, Harold. They'll let you out in the morning. You can be home for Christmas."

"The First Noel"

TRADITIONAL, MODERN VERSIONS CREDITED TO DAVIES GILBERT
RECORDED MAY 16, 1971

Although the title might suggest French origins for this classic, it's squarely an English folk song, likely dating back to the 1500s.

"The word *nowell* was first used by the famous fourteenth-century English poet Geoffrey Chaucer in his magnificent epic *The Canterbury Tales*, and it was a joyous shout on Christmas Day," wrote John M. Mulder and F. Morgan Roberts in their book *28 Carols to Sing at Christmas*. "'Nowell' probably comes from the old French word "noel," meaning Christmas, which comes from the Latin word 'natus' or 'birth.'"

Mulder and Roberts also note the biblical inaccuracy of the hymn, as scripture never mentions that shepherds saw "a star shining in the east" and, even if they had seen one, it would have meant they'd be swimming across the Mediterranean to visit Bethlehem. And with sheep, that would have been quite a feat.

Elvis and his predecessors, however, blow past any scriptural inaccuracies to deliver this carol's simple, hypnotic lullaby.

"The Lord can give . . . the Lord can take away," Elvis once said. "I might be herding sheep next year."

"On a Snowy Christmas Night"

WRITTEN BY STANLEY GELBER | RECORDED MAY 16, 1971

Songwriter Stan Gelber based the melody of *On a Snowy Christmas Night* on a fraternity song he wrote when he was twenty.

"Because it was a hymn, I always thought it sounded like it would work as a seasonal song," Gelber told writer Ken Sharp for the book *Elvis Presley: Writing for the King*. "I rewrote it as a Christmas lyric." In a twist of fate, Elvis recorded the song before his Hill & Range company could demand the publishing rights for "On a Snowy Christmas Night," thus neglecting a standard but usurious practice that favored Presley.

"This was a fluke and the Lord was on my side," Gelber said of the financial windfall.

He also loved the song, which has now appeared on multiple Christmas compilations by Elvis.

"Elvis did a magnificent job on the song," remembered Gelber. "The reason I love it is Elvis' rendition is heartfelt. The Imperials Quartet also enhanced the whole thing." Gelber penned one other song for Elvis, "My Desert Serenade," for the 1965 movie *Harum Scarum*.

Only one version of "On a Snowy Christmas Night" survives, as all the outtakes—along with the first six versions of "Winter Wonderland" on this record—were erased. Sadly, the same was true of the entirety of Elvis' first Christmas album from 1957. Due to mismanagement, many RCA tapes were erased or damaged, or went missing.

"Sure I go Christmas shopping! My mama and
I used to plan Christmas for days and we'd work out every
detail together. I enjoy it. Although the big revolving Christmas
tree that Mama loved so much has been stored away in the attic
at Graceland, it has to be replaced by a new one. The other one
broke. It has lots of sentiment for me for I always see my mother
sitting in the kitchen doorway in her chair looking at the tree
and loving the lights twinkling round and round as it turns
and the Christmas carols playing from the
music box in it. I intend to keep it."

—ELVIS PRESLEY (FROM *CHRISTMAS WITH ELVIS*
BY JIM CURTIN WITH RENATA GINTER, 1999)

"Winter Wonderland"

WRITTEN BY FELIX BERNARD AND RICHARD BERNHARD SMITH | RECORDED MAY 16, 1971

Again, Elvis enters Bing Crosby territory—was there a Christmas song Crosby didn't record?—with "Winter Wonderland." The Andrews Sisters and Perry Como also recorded popular versions of the tune, and it's since been covered by Bob Dylan, Dolly Parton, and Aretha Franklin, among others.

This particular recording was particularly tough for Elvis to pull off. After six takes and some jumbled lyrics, Elvis said with a laugh, "I'm getting tired of this damn song. Tired of it!"

He eventually got it, though, turning the song into a country music–tinged shuffle that you can still two-step to with your partner of choice.

"The Wonderful World of Christmas"

WRITTEN BY CHARLES TOBIAS AND AL FRISCH | RECORDED MAY 16, 1971

"The Wonderful World of Christmas" lyricist Charles Tobias also wrote "Don't Sit under the Apple Tree (with Anyone Else but Me)," recorded by Glenn Miller and the Andrews Sisters, and several songs for Nat King Cole, including "Miss You" and "Those Lazy-Hazy-Crazy Days of Summer." Tobias also cowrote "Merrily We Roll Along," the most famous theme of the Merrie Melodies cartoons with Bugs Bunny, Porky Pig, and the gang.

Tobias's gospel-inspired song also lent its title to Elvis' second Christmas album, *Elvis Sings the Wonderful World of Christmas*.

"If Elvis were alive today, he'd have gone back to his roots and he'd be singing gospel music," observed songwriter William Gaither.

"Elvis had so much emotion in his voice. There is a certain emotional quality that you have to have in your voice to connect with a gospel crowd. And he definitely had it. You can't put it into words," Gaither said.

ELVIS LOVED GRACELAND, IN PART, BECAUSE IT REMINDED HIM OF HIS MOTHER. He described to syndicated columnist May Mann the last Christmas with his mother in Graceland, calling it his "residence of the heart." He explained, "It is far more than a place of physical needs. . . . To me my home is all wound up with all the acts of kindness and gentleness that my mother and my grandmother and my daddy lovingly provided. . . . All of this love still remains within its walls. It's an enduring way of life for me."

"It Won't Seem Like Christmas (Without You)"

WRITTEN BY J. A. BALTHROP | RECORDED MAY 15, 1971

Elvis was a studio workhorse and this song proved to be a challenge. After Take 2 unraveled, Elvis kept plugging away. At one point, musician David Briggs banged away at his bell-piano (also called a celesta), which was meant to add a bit of church feeling to the proceedings—but Elvis added a line from "Merry Christmas Baby," mixing in some bluesy grit.

"I gotta hold you guys down, man," Elvis said, laughing.

Although Take 7 made it onto the record, Elvis' ad-lib as well as alternate takes can be heard on the double-CD, special edition version of *Elvis Sings the Wonderful World of Christmas*, released in 2011.

"I'll Be Home on Christmas Day"

WRITTEN BY MICHAEL JARRETT | RECORDED MAY 16, 1971, RE-RECORDED JUNE 10, 1971

In 1969, songwriter Michael Jarrett was going through a personal crisis. After fifteen years of toiling away in clubs six nights a week, he was "just burnt out," he remembered.

So Jarrett set his sights on Los Angeles—but threw himself a going-away party first. The bon voyage party crowd left his apartment so messy that a huge hunk of gravel lay on his shag carpet—or so he thought. On closer inspection, it wasn't gravel on his rug; it was a chunk of Afghan hash.

"I was so glad to find something to help me have an attitude adjustment," Jarrett remembered. "I was feeling so bad and didn't know what I was gonna do with my life."

So Jarrett fashioned an impromptu pipe from a coat hanger, smoked the hash, and started playing his guitar.

"I picked it up and it was Christmas Eve and I wrote 'I'll Be Home on Christmas Day' in ten minutes," he said. "It was life altering. The song was a gift."

Jarrett submitted two songs to Elvis—"I'll Be Home on Christmas Day" and "I'm Leavin'"—and the King of Rock 'n' Roll recorded both. After several takes of "I'll Be Home on Christmas Day," including one version that featured Jarrett's children, the song was shelved and re-recorded later in June.

A jovial, laughing Elvis broke up several times during the May recording session, bantering with producer Felton Jarvis and his backing band. He cut the verses, telling his crew, "Before we were doing eight verses, we'll cut it down to six."

After the band put some funk into Take 3, producer Jarvis playfully said, "That's a lot better like that, Elvis . . . that was too good."

However, these versions of "I'll Be Home on Christmas Day" were put into the vault, and the song was re-recorded a month later. It preceded the similarly named Tony Macaulay–penned "If I Get Home on Christmas Day" on side two of *Elvis Sings the Wonderful World of Christmas*.

"I'll Be Home on Christmas Day" also appears on the 1982 album *Memories of Christmas*, although alternate versions have been featured on *Platinum: A Life in Music* (1997) and *I Sing All Kinds* (2007). The song, along with several outtakes, was added to a deluxe edition of *Elvis Sings the Wonderful World of Christmas* (2011).

"If I Get Home on Christmas Day"

WRITTEN BY TONY MACAULAY | RECORDED MAY 15, 1971

Elvis' music publisher Freddy Bienstock commissioned songwriter Tony Macaulay for this tune. Macaulay, an Englishman, had previously written for the Foundations ("Baby, Now That I've Found You"), Andy Williams ("Home Lovin' Man"), and Long John Baldry ("Let the Heartaches Begin").

Macaulay had a peculiar way of getting into the skin of artists he was writing for.

"When I am asked to write a song for a famous act—I walk around the house being them for a day or so," he said. "I went around going 'Huh, huh, huh' and trying to be Elvis, which given my personal talent is no easy thing."

Like lyricist Kim Gannon on "I'll Be Home for Christmas," Macaulay tapped into the theme of longing for home during wartime.

"I wrote the song around the time of Vietnam and so it could be about a soldier coming home," Macaulay said. "The idea was maybe this song would appeal to all those people stuck in Vietnam in this completely unwinnable war."

Elvis hadn't fought in a war, but he had served in the military and knew what it was like to pine for home. From Germany in November of 1958, Elvis wrote to his friend Alan Fortas: "It's cold and there is nothing at all to do up here. I am about 200 miles from Friedberg and won't be back until the 20th of December. It will sure be a *great* Christmas this year. Ha! I would give almost anything to be home."

The original version of this song was more stripped-down and immediate sounding in the studio, although producer Felton Jarvis added what sounded like a full orchestra—complete with trumpets, backing vocals, and violins—to the final album version.

Macaulay might have preferred the original version over the overdubbed final product.

"It had a heavenly choir in it, which I didn't like much. It made it into this massive production and it lost all its intimacy for me," Macaulay said. "But it was Elvis doing it and it was on this Christmas album that sold millions so I was happy."

ELVIS CHRISTMAS MEMORIES

IN EARLY 1969, "ELVIS LOOKED LIKE HE WAS FEELING TEN CHRISTMASES ROLLED into one," remembered his friend George Klein. Not only was he riding high on the success of his televised comeback special, but he'd also celebrated his thirty-fourth birthday and welcomed his infant daughter, Lisa Marie Presley, on February 1.

"Holly Leaves and Christmas Trees"

WRITTEN BY GLENN SPREEN AND RED WEST | RECORDED MAY 15, 1971

Elvis met Red West in high school, and when Elvis became famous West was almost always at his side. West was there from the beginning and had learned to play guitar from Scotty Moore, who was part of Elvis' original band.

Later, West became a songwriter in his own right, penning songs for Pat Boone, Petula Clark, and Gary Puckett, as well as almost a dozen songs for Elvis. He also became an actor, and modern audiences might recognize him from *Road House* starring Patrick Swayze.

West ultimately wrote two Christmas songs for Elvis: "Holly Leaves and Christmas Trees" and "If Every Day Was Like Christmas."

Elvis liked singing gospel songs most, according to West, and used them to relax with his backup singers after his shows in Las Vegas.

"Gospel music is rock and roll with a religious flair," West said. "At the top of the Hilton, after the shows, the Stamps would come up and he'd sing gospel songs with them all night until dawn. This was wind down time."

"Merry Christmas Baby"

WRITTEN BY LOU BAXTER AND JOHNNY MOORE | RECORDED MAY 15, 1971

Johnny Moore's Three Blazers recorded this song in 1947 and it's since been covered by Elvis as well as Otis Redding, Christina Aguilera, Bruce Springsteen, CeeLo Green, Frankie Valli, Jeff Beck—and even Billy Idol.

Exactly who deserves credit for the song, however, has been a matter of contention. Charles Brown, the Three Blazers' singer and piano player, claimed that he had written the song.

For *Smithsonian* magazine, William Browning wrote: "Brown maintained that an ailing songwriter named Lou Baxter had asked him to record one of his songs as a favor, so he could pay for a throat operation. Brown said he reworked one of Baxter's compositions into 'Merry Christmas Baby' and recorded it with the Three Blazers. When the record came out, he said, he was surprised to see it credited to Baxter and Moore."

Through a bit of detective work, Browning discovered that "Lou Baxter" was a pseudonym for one Andrew Whitson Griffith, "an Army veteran in the dry-cleaning business who shopped lyrics around the Los Angeles blues scene in the 1940s and '50s."

Baxter/Griffith, Browning wrote, "deposited dozens of his songs in the US Copyright Office, including, in September 1947, one titled 'Merry Xmas Baby.' It was never published, but earlier this year, I laid eyes on a copy of the song from the Library of Congress. It was certainly the basis for 'Merry Christmas Baby'— the first verse is nearly identical to the song we know today, as is the second, rhyming 'music on the radio' with 'underneath the mistletoe.' After the start of the bridge, though, the lyrics chart a different course."

In the end, "Merry Christmas Baby" is a short, beautiful song with a long, complicated history.

"Silver Bells"

WRITTEN BY JAY LIVINGSTON AND RAY EVANS | RECORDED MAY 15, 1971

In a rehearsal before recording the song, Elvis asked his backing vocalists to help: "Charlie, why don't you guys do harmony with me and help me sing?"

After the harmonized version fell apart, Elvis performed it alone and brought the Christmas standard to life.

Bob Hope sang "Silver Bells" in the 1951 holiday film *The Lemon Drop Kid*, although the record by Bing Crosby would make the song a holiday staple. The original title for "Silver Bells" was "Tinkle Bells," but songwriter Ray Evans' wife thought it was too silly.

"The main reason this song became so successful is that this is the only song . . . that's about Christmas in a big city with shop lights and shoppers and the rest," remembered Evans. "We got that only because that happened to be the locale of the picture."

Although "Silver Bells" didn't win an Oscar, the songwriting team of Jay Livingston and Evans would take home three Academy Awards for Best Song of the Year, including 1948, 1950, and 1956. The last was for "Que Sera Sera" from Alfred Hitchcock's *The Man Who Knew Too Much*. Livingston and Evans also penned the theme song for the TV Western *Bonanza*, starring Lorne Greene and a young Michael Landon.

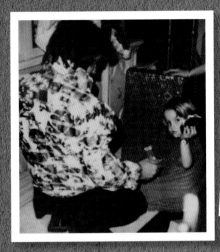

ELVIS' FIRST CHRISTMAS AS A FATHER WAS IN 1969. HIS OWN FATHER, VERNON, dressed up as Santa Claus for ten-month-old Lisa Marie.

"As always, Elvis and Priscilla had turned the Graceland grounds into a kind of winter wonderland, with sparkling lights strung up all through the property's magnificent oak trees, and a beautiful Christmas tree set up in the dining room," remembered friend George Klein.

Elvis rented out the Memphian Theatre in the week between Christmas and New Year's Day for a series of private movie screenings. What did Elvis show? The sex comedy *Candy* (1968), based on the novel by Terry Southern and Mason Hoffenberg. The farce starred Swedish actress Ewa Aulin in the title role, with appearances from Marlon Brando, Ringo Starr, John Huston, Richard Burton, and Walter Matthau, among others. The next year, he screened the Robert Redford movie *Little Fauss and Big Halsy*.

BONUS TRACK
"Mama Liked the Roses"

WRITTEN BY JOHNNY CHRISTOPHER | RECORDED JANUARY 15, 1969

Strictly speaking, "Mama Liked the Roses" isn't a Christmas song. In fact, it includes the words "Mother's Day" in the actual lyrics. However, it was released on the 1970 pressing of *Elvis' Christmas Album* and was one of Elvis' favorites, especially since it was written about his mother, so we'll give it some holiday love here.

In 1968, songwriter Johnny Christopher was playing bass for country singer Ronnie Milsap and had moved to Memphis, where he met Elvis after a club gig. Since they were both recording at American Studios, Christopher knew that he might be able to get a song in front of Elvis—but he didn't have one ready to go.

After staying up all night, Christopher had nothing. He went to bed at 7 a.m., only to wake up a half hour later to the words "mama liked the roses" ringing in his head.

"It was like a voice had spoken to me," Christopher said. "I thought, 'That's it! That's what I'm supposed to write.' I had never thought to write a song about Elvis' mother."

Within twenty minutes, Christopher had the bones of the song and finished it on a cocktail napkin the following night. Elvis loved the song and Christopher loved Elvis' rendition of it.

"Elvis really connected with the emotion of the song," Christopher said. "I was a young songwriter and musician, I might have been twenty-six at the time, and that was my first hit song and it was Elvis of all people. That song was a little miracle. . . . It just did not come from me, it came through me."

Elvis would also record a version of Christopher's "Always on My Mind" (previously recorded by B. J. Thomas), which Elvis cut in 1972 after his split with his wife, Priscilla. Ten years later, Willie Nelson's redefining rendition of "Always on My Mind" took home three Grammys for Song of the Year, Best Country Song, and Best Male Country Vocal Performance.

ELVIS' FAVORITE CHRISTMAS SONGS

FIRST AND FOREMOST, ELVIS WAS A MUSIC LOVER. FROM HIS CHILD-
hood, he revered artists such as Mississippi Slim, Dean Martin, and Hank
Williams, and later Roy Orbison and Tom Jones. He idolized gospel singer
Jake Hess, who worked with the Statesmen Quartet and the Imperials.

But what kind of Christmas music did Elvis listen to?

To answer this, we looked at his music collection stored at Graceland. Here's
what we found:

"Christmas Celebration"
by B. B. King

"Señor Santa Claus" by Jim Reeves

"The Christmas Song" by Nat King Cole

"If Every Day Was Like Christmas"
by Bobby West, aka Red West

"Merry Christmas"
by Don Tate and Larry McMillan

"A Little Boy's Christmas Prayer"
by Houston H. Loyd

"White Christmas" by Bing Crosby

ELVIS' CHRISTMAS MEMORIES

"Home means all the relatives
and friends getting together and all
of us talking and laughing and singing
and playing and enjoying ourselves.
Like Christmas, everyone was at Graceland.
And the boys, they have wives and
children and families, just everyone.
We had a great time. We had turkeys and a
huge Christmas tree, of course.
And lots of presents."

—ELVIS PRESLEY
(FROM *ELVIS AND THE COLONEL* BY MAY MANN, 1975)

CHRISTMAS 1954

A few days before Christmas 1954, Elvis and his small band were stopped for speeding after a show outside Shreveport, Louisiana.

Elvis told the *Commercial Appeal*: "It was cold, and I was sleepy. I woke up, and the officer asked, 'Who are you?' 'Elvis Presley, a singer.' The officer looked puzzled. Of course he had never heard of me. Hardly anyone had. I thought, 'Here goes my Christmas money for a traffic ticket.' But the officer let us go with a warning. . . . I gave a big sigh of relief.

"After the officer left, the three of us got out of the car and counted our money by the car headlights. The money was mostly in dollar bills. Man, that was the most money I ever had in my pockets at one time! I blew the whole bundle the next day for Christmas presents."

ELVIS PROPOSED TO PRISCILLA JUST BEFORE CHRISTMAS 1962 AND MADE THE announcement to his family on Christmas Eve.

Priscilla remembered that he entered her room with a boyish grin and his hands hidden behind his back. Elvis then asked her to close her eyes.

"When I opened my eyes, I found Elvis on his knees before me, holding a small black velvet box," Priscilla said. "I opened the box to find the most beautiful diamond ring I'd ever seen. It was three and a half carats encircled by a row of smaller diamonds, which were detachable—I could wear them separately. 'We're going to be married,' Elvis said."

FIREWORKS AT GRACELAND

In December 1957, Elvis was preparing to ship out for military service early the next year, and he wanted to go out with a bang. Quite literally.

On Christmas Eve, Elvis and his cousins piled into a limousine and crossed the state line into Mississippi, where fireworks were legally sold (fireworks were outlawed in Tennessee). The group hit four different fireworks shops, spending a total of $1,800—upward of $16,000 in today's money.

One clerk, after seeing Elvis' collection of rockets, buzz bombs, and Roman candles, asked, "What're you going to do? Start World War II all over again?"

"I'm thinking about it," Elvis said.

Back at Graceland, the press came calling.

"Elvis was in such a good mood he let reporters from the local newspaper come up to take pictures of him with his draft notice under the Christmas tree," his cousin Billy Smith recounted in Elaine Dundy's book *Elvis and Gladys*.

Once the reporters were gone, the fireworks came out. Elvis concocted a game he dubbed "War." The rules were simple: Two teams met up in the prairie behind Graceland to shoot fireworks at one another. The victors, it's assumed, had the fewest burn marks. The players grew savvier as the firefight became an annual tradition. They covered any exposed skin with heavy-duty "flight suits, racing helmets, goggles, and rags across our faces," remembered Elvis' step-brother David Stanley.

"Elvis loved fireworks," Stanley said. "Elvis would get a 12-pack of Roman candles and touch the whole thing off at once. He would become absolutely maniacal, running around . . . shooting fireworks at anyone in sight."

And when you got hit, you knew it.

"When one of the fireballs or rockets hit you, it gave you a pretty good lift and would sting like crazy," Smith remembered, "but we were having so much fun that no one seemed to mind."

The festivities, which could run as late as 4 a.m., were not without mishap. One year, one of Elvis' employees, Richard Davis, was hit by a buzz bomb that exploded in his face—melting his goggles around his eyes (he was ultimately okay). A couple of times, Graceland itself caught on fire and several cars were damaged when a stray fireball set off a box of fireworks in the carport.

"In the middle of all this, Elvis was rolling on the ground, laughing hysterically," Stanley said.

In 1957, Elvis' inebriated cousin Junior Smith was freshening up his cache of fireworks, only to drop his lighter into the munitions pile.

The hill "lit up like a Christmas tree," Smith said. "Boy! What a sight."

A stray rocket found its way into the henhouse. With feathers and sparks flying, Elvis said, "Mama is going to have a bunch of bald chickens."

In the small hours of the morning, the scorched group retired to Graceland.

"We sat downstairs in the basement den drinking sodas and reliving the game we had just finished," Smith remembered. "Elvis liked the game so much that it became an annual affair at Graceland."

ELVIS' CHRISTMAS NEAR-HIT, 1958

While stationed in Germany, Private First Class Elvis Presley bought himself a BMW 507 sports car a few days before Christmas—or so he thought. The all-white BMW, once owned by German race car driver Hans Stuck, was one of only 253 special models. But the contract Elvis signed, all in German, was a leasing agreement, not a purchasing agreement. When BMW requested the return of the 507, executives were upset that Elvis had the car painted red without permission, which was his solution to local girls constantly leaving him messages in lipstick on the white car.

After the initial December ceremony in which Elvis was presented the BMW keys, he didn't take delivery of the car, but his father Vernon drove him and his friends Lamar Fike and Red West back to Bad Nauheim, where they were renting a house.

"On the way home, they were hotly pursued by a photographer in another car," recounts Andreas Schröer in his book *Private Presley*. "In an attempt to shake him off, Vernon accelerated through a railroad crossing just as the gates were coming down. Unable to make it past the far gate before it lowered, the Mercedes and its occupants were trapped between it and the track just as the train was about to pass through. . . .Vernon managed to maneuver the car far enough away from the track for it to be left unscathed when the train roared past."

Just after Christmas, Elvis attended the *Holiday on Ice* show in nearby Frankfurt, Germany. He visited with the ice skaters, most of whom were American or British, and he was even photographed playfully "helping" one of the performers lace up her boots.

CHRISTMAS
CARDS
FROM ELVIS

Seasons Greetings
Elvis and
the colonel
and Friends

COLONEL TOM PARKER, THE CONSUMMATE BUSINESSMAN, MADE sure he and Elvis sent out a joint Christmas card each year, some of which spliced together pictures of the pair sporting holiday-themed costumes, including Parker dressed up as Santa. Here are a few samples from their yearly holiday greeting.

*Merry Christmas
and
Best Wishes
for the
New Year*

Elvis and the Colonel

May the
Wonderful Spirit
of Christmas
Bring Joy to You
and Yours

*

Elvis and the Colonel

"DIG THAT CRAZY SWISS BELL RINGER!"

To wish you a Cool Yule
and a Frantic First

ELVIS PRESLEY   COLONEL PARKER

TO THE WORLD

YOU PEACE AND HAPPINESS FOR

Christmas

AND THE NEW YEAR

HOLIDAY RECIPES FIT FOR THE KING OF ROCK 'N' ROLL

DESSERTS

ON THE KING OF ROCK 'N' ROLL'S CHRISTMAS TABLE, WE'VE ADDED some holiday favorites with Elvis' tastes in mind. The idea was to create a menu and party that Elvis himself would enjoy. So here you'll find holiday-themed light desserts (see Blue Christmas Pistachio Dessert and Snowy Christmas Lemon Squares) and heavy-duty sugar delivery devices (see Hunka Hunka Monster Christmas Cookies and No-Bake, All-Attitude Christmas Cookies) in quantities that will keep friends and family sated. You'll even have enough left over for Santa to take away in his big black Cadillac.

Hunka Hunka Monster Christmas Cookies

MAKES 10 TO 15 COOKIES, DEPENDING ON SIZE

Elvis' favorite foods included almost anything with peanut butter. So, with that in mind, we bring you the biggest peanut butter cookie we could find, complete with chocolate chips and brown sugar (which, honestly, sounds like a twelve-bar blues number).

3 eggs

1¼ cups packed brown sugar

1 cup granulated sugar

½ teaspoon salt

½ teaspoon vanilla extract

1 (12-ounce) jar creamy peanut butter

½ cup (1 stick) unsalted butter, softened

½ cup red and green M&M's (You'll need to buy two 10-ounce bags of M&M's to sort the colors.)

½ cup chocolate chips

2 teaspoons baking soda

4½ cups quick-cooking oats

Preheat the oven to 350°F.

In a large bowl, mix together the eggs and sugars. Add the salt, vanilla, peanut butter, and butter and combine. Stir in the M&M's, chocolate chips, baking soda, and oats. Drop by tablespoonfuls, 2 inches apart, onto cookie sheets covered in parchment paper or silicone baking mats.

Bake for 8 to 10 minutes. Do not overbake—the cookies should be soft. Leave them on the cookie sheets for about 3 minutes before transferring them to wire cooling racks. Don't forget to leave a few cookies out for Santa, although he might not be able to get back up the chimney after eating them.

Blue Christmas Pistachio Dessert

SERVES 10+ PEOPLE

If you spread the whipped topping *just* right on the top layer of this modern delicacy, you can imitate the curl of Elvis' 1956 dovetail haircut. This silky, smooth dessert is the peak of sweetness, so beware.

Crust
½ cup salted butter, melted

1 cup all-purpose flour

1 cup finely chopped walnuts or pecans

1 tablespoon granulated sugar

Filling, in three parts
THE FIRST LAYER (WHITE)

8 ounces cream cheese

3 cups whipped dessert topping (such as Cool Whip)

1 cup confectioners' sugar

THE SECOND LAYER (GREEN)

2 (3.4-ounce) packages instant pistachio pudding mix

3 cups whole milk

THE THIRD LAYER (BLUE)

5 drops blue food coloring (more may be needed to get desired color)

3 cups whipped dessert topping (such as Cool Whip)

Preheat the oven to 350°F.

In a medium bowl, mix together the crust ingredients with a pastry blender. Press the mixture into a 9 × 13-inch cake pan. Bake for 15 minutes. Let the crust cool.

In a large bowl, beat together the first layer of filling ingredients. Spread the mixture over the cooled crust.

In a medium bowl, mix the pistachio pudding with the milk (that's 1 less cup than the recipe on the box calls for). Spread this second layer over the cream cheese mixture.

In a medium bowl, mix the blue food coloring with the dessert topping. Slather this final layer over the green layer and don't forget the curl! Cool in the refrigerator for 2 hours. Put "Blue Christmas" on the hi-fi and enjoy.

AT GRACELAND, CHRISTMAS PRESENTS WERE OPENED ON CHRISTMAS EVE. THE house was decorated with a white plastic Christmas tree adorned with red ornaments, which matched Graceland's red velvet holiday curtains. The tree itself was futuristic: it slowly rotated and played Christmas music.

Snowy Christmas Lemon Squares

SERVES 10+ PEOPLE

These lemon bars are more than a powdered sugar platform, but feel free to go overboard on the snowlike powdered sugar in celebration of Elvis' favorite holiday.

Crust
2 cups all-purpose flour

1 cup (2 sticks) unsalted butter

½ cup confectioners' sugar

Filling and topping
4 large eggs

2 cups granulated sugar

¼ cup lemon juice

½ teaspoon salt

1 teaspoon baking powder

Confectioners' sugar, for sprinkling

Preheat the oven to 350°F.

Mix together the crust ingredients in a medium bowl. Pat the mixture into a 9 × 13-inch pan. Bake for 20 minutes. Let the crust cool.

In a medium bowl, beat together the eggs, sugar, lemon juice, salt, and baking powder for 3 minutes. Pour the mixture over the cooled crust. Bake for 25 minutes. Allow to cool before sprinkling confectioners' sugar over the bars. Cut the bars.

No-Bake, All-Attitude Christmas Cookies

MAKES ABOUT 20 COOKIES

Elvis would have loved that these peanut butter–based holiday cookies take care of business by being decadent and easy to make in a flash.

2 cups granulated sugar
½ cup whole milk
½ cup (1 stick) salted butter
¾ cup peanut butter
3 cups quick-cooking oats
5 tablespoons cocoa powder
1 teaspoon vanilla extract

Bring the sugar, milk, and butter to a boil for 1 minute in a small saucepan over medium heat.

Remove the saucepan from the stove and add the peanut butter, oatmeal, cocoa powder, and vanilla. Mix well, then allow to cool for 5 minutes.

Drop the dough by teaspoonfuls onto wax paper and roll into balls. Cool in the refrigerator for 10 minutes.

Serve and enjoy!

COCKTAILS

ADMITTEDLY, ELVIS WASN'T MUCH OF A DRINKER, ACCORDING TO his entourage and his dad, Vernon. He was more likely to enjoy a Coca-Cola and other soft drinks with friends.

"Gladys and I trusted him so completely that we'd go to a movie and let him have friends over for a party while we were gone," Vernon Presley told *Good Housekeeping* in 1978. "I expect there was some beer drinking that went on, but that's about as wild as it got. To tell you the truth, Elvis never did drink a lot. Although, once he about killed himself drinking peach brandy. He got a bottle and it tasted so good that he drank a little more and a little more until he'd drunk too much. But he was never a heavy drinker."

Still, we collected some traditional holiday and Southern cocktails that Elvis might have liked.

But definitely no peach brandy.

Bee's Knees

MAKES 1 DRINK

This cocktail was popular during Prohibition, when drinkers used honey and lemon juice to cover up the harshness of bathtub gin. But we've come a long way since the days of bathroom-distilled spirits, so let us suggest brands such as Beefeater, Tanqueray No. Ten, or Bombay Sapphire. A Bee's Knees drink pairs well with Snowy Christmas Lemon Squares (see page 114), although beware of the pucker power in that first sip after biting into a lemon square. It might curl your lip, just like Elvis'.

2 ounces gin

¾ ounce freshly squeezed lemon juice

½ ounce honey syrup (see note)

Lemon slice (or other fruit), for garnish

Add ice and the gin, lemon juice, and honey syrup to a shaker and shake well. Then strain the mixture into a cocktail glass. Top it off with a lemon slice or other garnish.

NOTE: You can make your own honey syrup by adding ½ cup of honey to ½ cup of water in a saucepan over medium heat. Cook until it reaches desired consistency and add more honey as desired for sweetness and personal taste.

Brandy Milk Punch

MAKES 1 DRINK

This holiday cocktail has its roots in seventeenth-century England, but it has found an enthusiastic fan base in the American South. Brandy Milk Punch— a cousin to Christmas favorite eggnog and a sibling to the rum-based Tom and Jerry—is a creamy, dreamy classic recipe that will make you feel warm and fuzzy as the extended version of "Merry Christmas Baby" plays softly in the background. Try pairing with our Hunka Hunka Monster Christmas Cookies (see page 111) for that classic milk-and-cookies experience.

1 ounce rum

2 ounces cognac

1½ ounces whole milk

2 teaspoons granulated sugar

Nutmeg, for garnish

Fill a tumbler halfway with crushed (or shaved) ice and add the rum, cognac, milk, and sugar, along with 2 teaspoons of water. Shake well. Then strain the mixture into a cocktail glass. Add a sprinkle of nutmeg for holiday flavor.

Christmas Mimosa

MAKES 1 DRINK

A holiday spin on a brunch classic, the Christmas Mimosa will add sweetness and a ruby-colored flair to your next holiday party.

½ cup Champagne
(or sparkling wine)
2 tablespoons cranberry juice

Pour the Champagne over the cranberry juice in a festive flute.

NOTE: To add more tart sweetness to the drink, substitute 2 tablespoons of pomegranate juice and a sugar cube for the cranberry juice. If you go with this variant, make sure to place the sugar cube in the glass first.

IN THE 1960S, ELVIS ANNOUNCED AN UNSCHEDULED VISIT TO GRACELAND FROM California, where he was making movies.

"He loved Christmas so much that one year he telephoned . . . and instructed the yard man to put lights all around the drive," remembered his secretary Becky Yancey. "They worked all day and half the night to get the job completed before Elvis arrived home at four o'clock in the morning. He was so pleased that he parked across Elvis Presley Boulevard and sat in the car, looking at the display for several minutes before driving onto the mansion grounds."

One Christmas, friend George Klein gave Elvis a black leather rolling book-case with "EP" written in white on the doors.

"There was always trouble finding a way to pack and organize the pile of books he wanted to bring with him," Klein remembered. "When he opened it up that Christmas Eve, his eyes lit up like a kid's. He stopped the whole process of gift-giving and gift-opening and had somebody go up to his bedroom and bring down a stack of books so he could test it out."

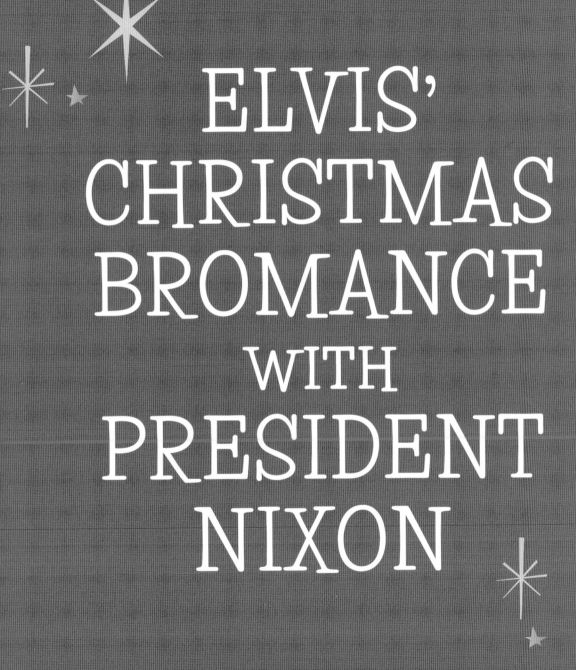

ELVIS' CHRISTMAS BROMANCE WITH PRESIDENT NIXON

*I*N 1970, AFTER AN ARGUMENT WITH HIS FATHER AND PRISCILLA ABOUT the extravagant amount of money—more than $100,000—that he spent on luxury cars and firearms that holiday season, Elvis stormed out of Graceland and headed to the airport. Taking what were his first-ever commercial flights, Elvis ended up in Washington, DC.

Elvis, who had begun collecting police badges, decided that what he really wanted—for Christmas or otherwise—was a badge from the Bureau of Narcotics and Dangerous Drugs.

So, naturally, he wrote the commander in chief himself, President Richard M. Nixon. "I am Elvis Presley and admire you and have great respect for your office. . . . Sir, I can and will be of any service that I can to help the country out," Elvis wrote in his uneven penmanship.

On American Airlines stationery, Elvis wrote, "The drug culture, the hippie elements, . . . Black Panthers, etc. do not consider me as their enemy," and he offered to go undercover as a federal agent at large to help the president.

To Elvis, Priscilla later wrote, such a badge "represented some kind of ultimate power. . . . With the federal narcotics badge, he [believed he] could legally enter any country both wearing guns and carrying any drugs he wished."

Handing his letter off to the guard at the White House at 6:30 a.m., Elvis then went to the Washington Hotel, where he was staying under the alias Jon Burrows.

And the president called. Or rather, his aide Egil "Bud" Krogh did. Krogh was an Elvis fan and talked his bosses into setting up a meeting with the King of Rock 'n' Roll.

On December 21, 1970, Elvis entered the Oval Office in a purple velvet suit and amber sunglasses, greeting President Nixon with the gift of a World War II Colt .45 pistol displayed in a glass case.

Although there was no audio recording of the meeting, several accounts survive.

When Nixon looked at Presley's attire—including a massive, diamond-encrusted, gold-plated belt buckle—the president said, "You dress kind of wild, don't you, son?"

Without missing a beat, Elvis said, "Mr. President, you've got your show to run and I've got mine," and both men laughed.

The pair took photos together and chatted for about a half hour about the problems the country faced.

As the meeting wrapped up, Nixon asked his aide if the White House could provide Elvis with a badge. In response, Elvis unexpectedly hugged the president with his left arm, saying, "Thank you very much, sir. This means a lot to me." After lunch in the White House commissary, Krogh presented Elvis with his much-sought-after narcotics badge—which was largely ceremonial, although Elvis didn't seem to notice or care.

Elvis looked "like a kid who'd just received all of the Christmas presents he'd asked for," remembered Krogh later.

Nixon gave him what Santa could not.

GIFTS
AND
ELVIS

ELVIS WAS A CREATIVE, OVER-THE-TOP GIVER OF GIFTS, AND CHRISTMAS was his opportunity to thank his staff and let his family know that he loved them with piles of presents. Here's a list of just a few of the items (and pets) that Elvis gave over the holidays:

In 1955, Elvis visited his old high school, L. C. Humes, and gave one of his teachers, Mrs. Scrivener, an electric alarm clock.

In 1955, Elvis bought his girlfriend Dixie Locke a pair of shorts and a pink, sleeveless blouse.

In 1957, Elvis bought his manager, Colonel Tom Parker, a red Isetta sports car.

In 1959, Elvis bought a gold wristwatch with a diamond for Priscilla.

In 1962, Elvis bought a poodle for Priscilla, which she named Honey.

In 1964, Elvis bought a new wheelchair for Gary Pepper, one of Elvis' earliest fans and president of his fan club.

In 1966, Elvis bought horses for Priscilla and friend Sandy Kawelo.

In 1967, Elvis gave a $595 Accutron watch to Colonel Tom Parker, and a watch to the Colonel's lieutenant, Tom Diskin.

In 1968, Elvis gave friends and staff $100 and $200 gift vouchers from Goldsmith's department store.

In 1970, Elvis bought three Mercedes: one for himself and one each for his girlfriend Barbara Leigh and his friend Jerry Schilling.

In 1972, Elvis bought girlfriend Linda Thompson a mink coat and a fox suede coat.

In 1976, Elvis bought Lisa Marie a customized baby-blue Harley golf cart with her name and a rose painted on the side.

IN 1971, CITING "A MIGHTY LEAN YEAR," ELVIS GAVE CHRISTMAS ENVELOPES TO his staff with fifty-cent McDonald's gift certificates. After the joke met with silence, Elvis jovially gave out "real gifts which included envelopes stuffed with cash for his employees," wrote Peter Guralnick.

WHAT DO YOU BUY FOR AN INTERNATIONAL SUPERSTAR WHO almost literally has everything?

"For a guy who could buy anything he wanted for himself, Christmas presents were a big deal to Elvis," remembered friend George Klein. "He didn't care what you gave him, but he wanted to get something."

So here are a few things friends, fans, and family gave to Elvis:

In 1957, Elvis' girlfriend Barbara Hearn bought him a gold lamé vest, which he wore on *The Ed Sullivan Show*.

In 1958, in Germany, Elvis' father, Vernon, gave him an electric guitar.

In 1959, Priscilla gave Elvis a set of bongo drums.

In 1962, Priscilla gave Elvis a musical cigarette box that played "Surrender."

In 1965, Elvis' entourage gave him a four-foot statue of Jesus with his arms outstretched for Graceland's meditation garden. "I carved it in the front living room; it's the world's largest plastic Jesus (they [still] think it's marble)," said sculptor John McIntire.

In the mid-1960s, Elvis received a giant starburst clock from friend George Klein, which still hangs over the mantle at Graceland.

In the 1960s, Priscilla gave Elvis a slot-car track.

In 1970, Elvis wore the black "fur-cloth" bell-bottom suit that Priscilla had given him to attend friend Sonny West's wedding, where he served as best man on December 28.

In 1976, Elvis's girlfriend Ginger Alden bought him a large gold-chain necklace, which held a tiger's eye gemstone at the center of a crucifix.

Fans sent Elvis "dozen of shirts . . . usually the right size. He received piles of handkerchiefs, billfolds, key chains, cufflinks, neckties he never wore, and gallons of shaving lotion. An affluent and more imaginative fan once sent him a gold toothpick," wrote his secretary, Becky Yancey, in her book *My Life with Elvis*. "Some fans fashioned their own presents for him, knitting sweaters, caps, and socks."

Employees pooled their money, Yancey remembered, to buy gifts "such as a Bible dictionary, pajamas, book ends, leather gloves, clothes hangers, pipes, and cologne."

You read that right. Someone had the temerity (or thoughtful foresight) to buy Elvis hangers for Christmas.

SELECTED BIBLIOGRAPHY

Adams, Nick. *The Rebel & the King*. WaterDancer Press, 2012.

Alden, Ginger. *Elvis & Ginger: Elvis Presley's Fiancée and Last Love Finally Tells Her Story*. New York: Penguin, 2014.

Anderson, Nancy. "Elvis: By His Father Vernon Presley." *Good Housekeeping*, January 1978.

Becker, Peter. "Local History: Winter Wonderland's Team: Dick Smith & Felix Bernard." *Tri-county Independent*, December 19, 2016. www.tricountyindependent. com/news/20161219/local-history-winter-wonderlands-team-dick-smith--felix-bernard.

Bergreen, Laurence. *As Thousands Cheer: The Life of Irving Berlin*. New York: Hachette Books, 1990.

Billboard. Accessed June 3, 2020. https://www.billboard.com.

Binder, Steve. *Comeback '68 | Elvis: The Story of the Elvis Special*. Meteor 17, 2018.

Brown, Bennett. "Classic Cocktail Guide." *Edible Memphis*, October 20, 2019. www.ediblememphis.com/stories/classic-cocktail-guide.

Brown, Shane. "Elvis Presley, Irving Berlin and White Christmas." *Beyond Boundaries* (blog), August 31, 2016. silentmovieblog.wordpress.com/2015/11/29/elvis-presley-irving-berlin-and-white-christmas/.

Browning, William. "Who Really Wrote 'Merry Christmas, Baby.'" *Smithsonian*, November 1, 2017. www.smithsonianmag.com/arts-culture/who-wrote-merry-christmas-baby-180965207/.

Bush, John. Review of *Christmas Duets* by Elvis Presley. AllMusic. www.allmusic.com/album/christmas-duets-mw0000799719.

Collins, Ace. *More Stories behind the Best-Loved Song of Christmas*. Grand Rapids, MI: Zondervan, 2006.

———. *Stories behind the Best-Loved Song of Christmas*. Grand Rapids, MI: Zondervan, 2001.

———. *Untold Gold: The Stories behind Elvis' #1 Hits*. Chicago: Chicago Review Press, 2005.

Crouch, Kevin, and Tanja Crouch. *The Gospel according to Elvis*. London: Bobcat Books, 2007.

Curtin, Jim, and Renata Ginter. *Christmas with Elvis*. Nashville: Celebrity Books, 1999.

Dundy, Elaine. *Elvis and Gladys*. Jackson, MS: University Press of Mississippi, 2004.

Eder, Mike. *Elvis Music FAQ: All That's Left to Know about the King's Recorded Works*. London: Backbeat Books, 2013.

Elvis Australia. "Elvis Still Holds Top-Selling USA Christmas Album." Elvis Australia: Official Elvis Presley Fan Club, December 24, 2008. www.elvis.com.au/presley/news/top-selling-christmas-albums-208.shtml.

ElvisNews.com. "Original Graceland Nativity Scene on eBay." ElvisNews.com, updated December 22, 2007. https://www.elvisnews.com/news.aspx/original-graceland-nativity-scene-on-ebay/10140.

———. "Gene Autry Turner Presented Elvis Presley with Sheriff's Badge" (includes commentary by Gene Autry Turner). YouTube video, 3:02. June 9, 2014. https://www.youtube.com/watch?v=Sdg724_3z-o.

Gaar, Gillian G. *100 Things Elvis Fans Should Know & Do Before They Die*. Chicago: Triumph Books, 2014.

Goldman, Albert. *Elvis*. New York: McGraw-Hill, 1981.

Graceland. "Gates of Graceland—Elvis and Graceland at Christmas." Graceland.com. YouTube video, 12:28. December 28, 2015.

Graves, Michael P., and David Fillingim, eds. *More Than Precious Memories: The Rhetoric of Southern Gospel Music*. Macon, GA: Mercer University Press, 2004.

Grudens, Richard. *Jukebox Saturday Night: More Memories of the Big Band Era and Beyond*. Saint James, NY: Celebrity Profiles, 1999.

Guralnick, Peter. *Careless Love: The Unmaking of Elvis Presley*. New York: Abacus, 2013.

———. *Last Train to Memphis: The Rise of Elvis Presley*. New York: Little, Brown, 1994. Kindle Edition.

Guralnick, Peter, and Ernst Jorgensen. *Elvis Day by Day: The Definitive Record of His Life and Music*. New York: Ballantine Books, 1999.

———. Liner notes and discography from *The Complete Elvis Presley Masters*. RCA Legacy, 2010.

Hawn, Michael. "History of Hymns: 'O Little Town of Bethlehem.'" Discipleship Ministries, United Methodist Church, June 14, 2013. www.umcdiscipleship.org/resources/history-of-hymns-o-little-town-of-bethlehem.

History.com Editors. "Elvis Presley Is Drafted." History.com, December 20, 2019. www.history.com/this-day-in-history/elvis-presley-is-drafted.

Horstman, Dorothy. *Sing Your Heart Out, Country Boy*. Nashville: Country Music Foundation, 1976.

IMDb. Accessed June 10, 2020. www.imdb.com/?ref_=nv_home.

Jorgensen, Ernst. *Elvis Presley: A Life in Music; The Complete Recording Sessions*. New York: St. Martin's Press, 1998.

Klein, George, and Chuck Crisafulli. *Elvis: My Best Man; Radio Days, Rock 'n' Roll Nights, and My Lifelong Friendship with Elvis Presley*. New York: Crown, 2010.

Knorr, Paul. *Big Bad-Ass Book of Cocktails: 1,500 Recipes to Mix It Up!* Philadelphia: Running Press, 2010.

"Kurt Russell / Claire Foy / David Walliams / Lee Evans / Mumford and Sons." *The Graham Norton Show*. Season 24, episode 6. Written by Rob Colley and Christine Rose, directed by Steven Smith. BBC One, November 2, 2018.

Lambert, Arden. "'Peace in the Valley': Red Foley's Version That Made It to the Chart." *Country Thang Daily*, November 2, 2019. www.countrythangdaily.com/peace-valley-foley-version/.

Larkin, Colin. *The Encyclopedia of Popular Music*. London: Omnibus Press, 2011.

Latham, Caroline, and Jeannie Sakol. *"E" Is for Elvis: An A-to-Z Guide to the King of Rock and Roll*. New York: NAL Books, 1990.

LeDonne, Rob. "'White Christmas' at 75: A Snapshot of the Most Successful Song in Music History." *Billboard*, December 20 2017. www.billboard.com/articles/news/holiday/8071111/white-christmas-bing-crosby-history.

Leiber, Jerry, and Mike Stoller. *Hound Dog: The Leiber & Stoller Autobiography*. New York: Simon & Schuster, 2010.

Leigh, Spencer. *Elvis Presley: Caught in a Trap*. Carmarthen, Wales: McNidder & Grace, 2017.

Liquor.com. "Classics You Should Know: The Bee's Knees." Liquor.com. www.liquor.com/recipes/bees-knees/.

McAllister Linn, Brian. *Elvis's Army: Cold War GIs and the Atomic Battlefield*. Cambridge, MA: Harvard University Press, 2016.

McKeon, Elizabeth, and Linda Everett. *Elvis Speaks*. Nashville: Cumberland House, 2004.

McLafferty, Clair. "5 Essentials: Cocktails Every Southerner Should Master." *The Bitter Southerner*. bittersoutherner.com/the-5-essentially-southern-cocktails.

Mulder, John M., and F. Morgan Roberts. *28 Carols to Sing at Christmas*. Eugene, OR: Cascade Books, 2015.

Mulligan, Hugh. "Elvis Christmas Album Seen Masterpiece of Miscasting." Associated Press. Printed in *Ottawa Citizen*, December 14, 1957, p. 30.

Myers, Justin. "The Songs That Spent the Longest at Number 1." Official Charts, the Official UK Charts Company, December 13, 2019. www.officialcharts.com/chart-news/the-songs-that-spent-the-longest-at-number-1_14522/.

Nobbman, Dale V. *Christmas Music Companion Fact Book: The Chronological History of Our Most Well-Known Traditional Christmas Hymns, Carols, Songs and the Writers & Composers Who Created Them*. Anaheim, CA: Centerstream, 2000.

NPR. "'White Christmas.'" *All Things Considered*, December 25, 2000. www.npr.org/2000/12/25/1116021/white-christmas.

Official Charts. "'Santa Bring My Baby Back To Me': Full Official Chart History." Official Charts, 2020. www.officialcharts.com/search/singles/santa-bring-my-baby-back-to-me/.

Osborne, Jerry. *Elvis: Word for Word*. New York: Gramercy Books, 2000.

Pierce, Patricia Jobe. *The Ultimate Elvis: Elvis Presley Day by Day*. New York: Simon & Schuster, 1994.

Presley, Dee, Billy Stanley, Rick Stanley, David Stanley, and Martin Torgoff. *Elvis: We Love You Tender*. New York: Delacorte Press, 1979.

Presley, Elvis. *The Complete Elvis Presley Masters*. RCA Legacy, 2010.

———. *Elvis' Christmas Album*. RCA / Follow That Dream Records, 2014.

———. *Elvis: Memories of Christmas*. RCA, 1987.

———. *Elvis Sings the Wonderful World of Christmas*. RCA / Follow That Dream Records, 2011.

———. *Elvis '68 Comeback Special*. Deluxe ed. DVD. NBC/BMG/RCA, Elvis Presley Enterprises, 2004.

———. *If Every Day Was Like Christmas*. Limited ed. RCA, 1994.

Presley, Priscilla Beaulieu, and Sandra Harmon. *Elvis and Me*. New York: G. P. Putnam's Sons, 1985.

Saulovich, Johnny. Liner notes from *Elvis' Christmas Album*. RCA / Follow That Dream Records, 2014.

Schilling, Jerry, and Chuck Crisafulli. *Me and a Guy Named Elvis: My Lifelong Friendship with Elvis Presley*. New York: Viking, 2008.

Schröer, Andreas. *Private Presley: The Missing Years; Elvis in Germany*. New York: William Morrow, 1993.

Scott, Brian. *But Do You Recall? 25 Days of Christmas Carols and the Stories behind Them*. Lulu.com, 2015.

Second Hand Songs. "Santa Claus Is Back in Town." Second Hand Songs: A Cover Songs Database, Retrieved 2020. secondhandsongs.com/performance/78119.

Sharp, Ken. *Elvis Presley: Writing for the King*. New York: FTD Books, 2006.

Songfacts. "'Blue Christmas' by Elvis Presley: Songfacts." Songfacts, 2020. https://www.songfacts.com/facts/elvis-presley/blue-christmas.

——. "'Santa Claus Is Back in Town' by Elvis Presley: Songfacts." Songfacts, 2020. https://www.songfacts.com/facts/elvis-presley/santa-claus-is-back-in-town.

Stanley, Billy, and George Erikson. *Elvis, My Brother*. New York: St. Martin's Press, 1989.

Stanley, David, and David Wimbish. *Life with Elvis*. Old Tappan, NJ: Fleming H. Revell, 1986.

Tagliaferre, Lewis. *Theofatalism: Theology for Agnostics and Atheists*. Bloomington, IN: iUniverse, 2013.

Tsort. "Song Artist 2—Elvis Presley." Tsort, 2019. tsort.info/music/mfeulb.htm.

Victor, Adam. *The Elvis Encyclopedia*. New York: Overlook Duckworth, 2008.

Ward, Mark, Sr. *The Lord's Radio: Gospel Music Broadcasting and the Making of Evangelical Culture, 1920–1960*. Jefferson, NC: McFarland & Company, 2017.

Whiteley, Sheila. *Christmas, Ideology and Popular Culture*. Edinburgh, Scotland: Edinburgh University Press, 2008.

Williamson, Joel, and Donald Lewis Shaw. *Elvis Presley: A Southern Life*. Oxford, England: Oxford University Press, 2015.

WMC-TV. "Elvis Had Decorations Custom Made for Graceland." WMC-TV, December 18, 2012. https://www.wmcactionnews5.com/story/20368241/an-exclusive-look-at-christmas-with-the-king/.

Wolfe, Charles. Liner notes from *If Every Day Was Like Christmas*. Limited ed. RCA, 1994.

Yancey, Becky, and Cliff Linedecker. *My Life with Elvis*. New York: St. Martin's Press, 1977.

Zollo, Paul. *More Songwriters on Songwriting*. Boston, MA: Da Capo Press, 2016.

ACKNOWLEDGMENTS

THIS BOOK WOULDN'T HAVE BEEN POSSIBLE WITHOUT MY INDUSTRIOUS editors, Jordana Hawkins and Jennifer Leczkowski, and my longtime friend and agent, David Dunton. (And thanks to Jennifer Kasius for suggesting me for the project in the first place.)

My assistants Madeline Knathaus and Lejla Subasic helped me hunt down little-known Elvis facts and scoured databases for every Elvis Christmas tidbit we could find. Thanks also to Ken Sharp, who wrote the amazing book *Writing for the King*, for his kindness and generosity. Also: a shout of gratitude to Angie Marchese, vice president of archives and exhibits at Elvis Presley Enterprises, for her support. Thanks to Chris King, who brought Elvis to life with his amazing illustrations.

Special thanks to Scott and Holly Stratford (my godfather and his wife), who lent us their condo in Bozeman, Montana, where half of this book was written in a paradise without Wi-Fi (although that may be redundant). We're still sorry about the busted garbage disposal. And your DVD of *A River Runs through It*.

Thanks to my friend Suzanna Naramore, who would famously bring her Elvis Christmas CD to work every year—until it went missing. When it magically appeared in the office the next year, she stole it back, returning Elvis to his rock 'n' roll throne.

Thanks to my friend Peter Guralnick, the King of Elvis Biographers, for his good humor and good taste. Jennifer Greenstein did a heroic job of copy editing the manuscript, and I'm forever indebted. Amanda Richmond proved herself to be the queen of book design.

Lastly, my wife, Betsy—a paragon of support and patience—provided me with essential editing and feedback when I needed it most. So thanks to my hunka burnin' love, who will be embarrassed when she reads this sentence.

PHOTO CREDITS

ABOUT THE AUTHOR

ROBERT K. ELDER IS THE AUTHOR OF FOURTEEN BOOKS, INCLUDING
Read Your Partner Like a Book, The Mixtape of My Life, and *Hidden Hemingway.* His work has appeared in the *New York Times,* the *Los Angeles Times,* the *Boston Globe,* the *Paris Review,* and many other publications. He is the chief digital officer for the Bulletin of the Atomic Scientists and the founder of Odd Hours Media. Robert lives and writes in Chicagoland. Visit him on Twitter at @robertkelder and on his website at www.robertkelder.com.